Championship Teams of the NFL

In this book Phil Berger tells the stories of the players and the coaches of six outstanding teams that fought thrilling uphill battles for the N.F.L. title: Chicago Bears (1940), Los Angeles Rams (1951), New York Giants (1956), Baltimore Colts (1958), Green Bay Packers (1961) and Cleveland Browns (1964).

Championship Teams of the NFL

by Phil Berger

Illustrated with photographs and diagrams

Random House   New York

Photograph credits: Vernon J. Biever, cover, 92, 115, 124-125, 128, 129, 132, 137; Malcolm Emmons, 147, 149, 158, 169; Fred Roe, front endpaper, v, vi, x-xi, back endpaper; UPI, 8, 13, 17, 23, 26-27, 29, 33, 46-47, 51, 53, 55, 57, 67, 70, 71, 80, 82-83, 95, 98, 100, 103, 104, 112, 143, 160, 162, 167; Wide World, 43, 75, 110, 153

Library of Congress Catalog Card Number: 68-23667

Manufactured in the United States of America

To my old touch-football buddies
AL LEVINE and BILL GUTMAN

CONTENTS

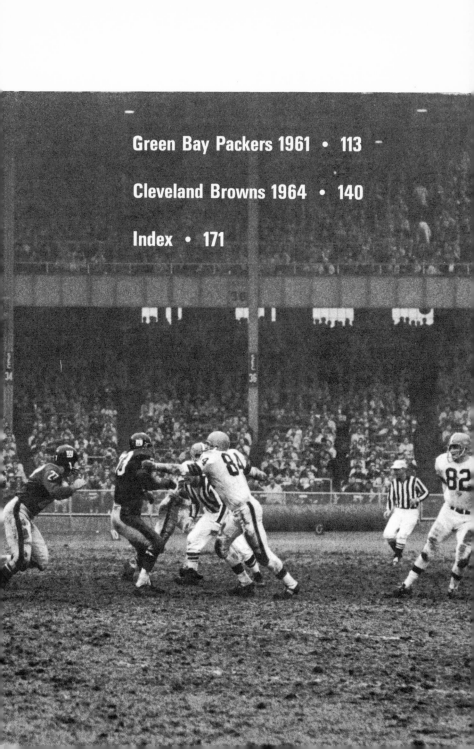

Championship Teams of the NFL

CHICAGO
BEARS
1940

Professional football in its early days was not the multi-million dollar business it is today. When the first pro league, the American Professional Football League, was formed in 1920, a franchise cost only $100. Most teams in the organization did not come from big cities. For pro football at the time was a small-town game played mainly in the coal and steel districts of America.

Among the charter members in the APFL were the Decatur (Illinois) Staleys. The name Staleys came from a Decatur manufacturer, the A. E. Staley Starch Company. Though few people today recall the Staleys, the team's role in football history is important. It was the forerunner of one of the great National Football League clubs, the Chicago Bears.

When the name of the American Professional Football League was changed to the National Football League in 1922, the Staleys had already left Decatur to become the Chicago Bears. Under Coach George Halas, they immediately became one of the most feared teams in the league.

By the end of 1938, however, the rest of the league no longer feared the Bears, who had slumped to third place after winning the Western Division title only the year before. And a further decline seemed likely. But at the end of the 1938 season Halas made a decision that he felt would put the Bears in contention once again.

In an era when football teams ran the ball almost every play, most pro coaches preferred the single-wing offense. But Halas planned to replace his single-wing system with the *T*-formation, an offensive setup the pros had used infrequently for a number of years.

The single wing is primarily a running formation. Its principal strength is the weight of blockers it provides ahead of the runner. The key man, the tailback, usually stands five to six yards behind the center. When the ball is snapped to him, he can either run or pass. Generally, he runs, and then the other backs can give him a fine blocking escort. The single wing is a simple power formation and the other team's defenses do not have trouble seeing the play develop. Their only problem is to

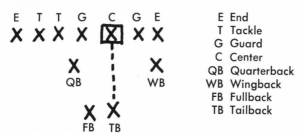

SINGLE WING

In the single wing the tailback, who is the key man, plays behind the center, but he is five yards back.

stop force with force. Today, the single wing is used only by scattered high school and college teams that still favor the rushing game.

The *T*-formation is more complex. The quarterback takes the snap directly from the center, and plays can be executed before a defense can adjust properly. The *T* allows for a quicker, more balanced attack, and it is as suitable for passing as for running. The *T* also has the advantage of being a much more deceptive offensive arrangement than the single wing.

Once Halas decided to revise his system, he began to look for a quarterback. The quarterback was the most important player in the *T*-formation, just as he is in pro ball today. He had to call the plays and handle the ball on every down. He could give the ball to the other backs, run or pass it himself. A good quarterback would be the spark plug of Halas' *T*-formation.

T FORMATION

E T G C G T E
X X X ⊠ X X X   QB Quarterback
       XQB   HB Halfback
                             FB Fullback
HB FB HB
X X X

This is the basic *T* of Halas' day. The quarterback, who is the key man, plays directly behind the center. Often, one end is "split"— that is, he is separated from the other linemen by six or more yards.

Also, one of the backs may be "flanked."

X X X ⊠ X X   X SE   SE Split End
      X   X FB   FB Flankerback
    X X

Strangely enough, the man Halas picked as his quarterback had no experience in the *T*-formation, besides never having played pro football. Instead, Sid Luckman had been a single-wing tailback at Columbia University. Although the tailback's moves required a different pattern of physical movements, the Bear coach believed that Luckman had the intelligence and dedication to master the complexities of the *T*.

Halas knew his man—Luckman *was* dedicated. Before entering college Sid had been offered scholarships by several top football schools, but he had turned them down. He wanted an education more than athletic glory. Fortunately, Columbia University coach Lou Little stressed the importance of an education, and he offered Sid the challenge of working hard for everything he got. Luckman was sold on Columbia and went there without a scholarship.

During his freshman year, his work schedule was demanding. In addition to his studies, Luckman washed dishes for two hours a day to earn his meals, and worked as a messenger boy and scrubbed walls for spending money. He was so busy that he did not play football during his first year.

When he finally went out for the team, he became a star tailback. Halas heard of Luckman and went to see him play in 1938, Sid's senior year. "When I first saw Sid at Columbia that afternoon, playing Cornell in the rain," Halas later recalled, "I knew I had the quarterback I wanted."

When Luckman first joined the Bears, however, he was not as certain of his abilities as his coach. As a single-wing tailback in college, he had been a natural. But the *T*-formation was more difficult, and Sid was required to know every player's maneuvers in each of the Bears' 400 plays. It was a staggering learning chore, but Sid studied his play book alone in his room at night until he could recite it from memory.

That was only one of Luckman's problems, however. He also had to learn his moves as a quarterback. Although he couldn't learn everything right away, he worked hard to improve. He practiced the new moves hour after hour on the field, and for more hours at night, pivoting before a mirror.

His attitude was good. He paid attention to the coaches, particularly Assistant Coach Clark Shaughnessy. Shaughnessy had been a single-wing coach at the University of Chicago in the late 1930s. But he had devoted much of his time there to developing the full potential of the *T* on paper. He had worked out many blocking combinations which were then unique to the game. (Previously, a lineman had simply blocked the opponent oppo-

Coach Halas and his new quarterback, Sid Luckman, work out a T-*formation play.*

site him. Shaughnessy had modified this to include plays in which linemen also "criss-crossed" and "double-teamed" on blocks.) Sid absorbed the instructions of his coaches, and in time he could do everything reasonably well in practice.

But Halas had to make sure that Luckman could quarterback under game conditions. To allow Sid to adjust to the new position gradually, the Bear coach alternated him between left halfback and quarterback during the 1939 season. Sid showed enough progress to take over the job in the memorable 1940 season.

The rest of the team also showed progress. In the two years following the Bears' third-place finish in 1938, Halas had assembled a group that would eventually be remembered by football fans as "The Monsters of the Midway."

In the backfield with Luckman were fullback Bill Osmanski and halfbacks Ray Nolting and rookie George McAfee. All were highly competent runners, especially McAfee. At Duke he had run the 100-yard dash in 9.7 seconds. During the football season, he built up his speed in a unique way. In practice sessions throughout the week, McAfee wore regulation football shoes. On game Sundays, he shed them for lightweight oxfords. This method of training resulted in increased speed and maneuverability and helped him to become the Bears' most dangerous runner.

Naturally, McAfee had help from the Bear linemen. The star of Chicago's forward wall was another rookie, center Clyde "Bulldog" Turner. Turner had been a late developer. When he was graduated from high school in Sweetwater, Texas, he weighed only 160 pounds. His size did not attract much attention, and not one college offered him a football scholarship. So Turner enrolled at Hardin-Simmons University in Abilene, Texas. In time, the little fellow who had been too skinny and baby-faced to excite college scouts grew to a height of 6 feet 1 inch and weighed 235 pounds. He also became a rugged football player and starred at Hardin-Simmons. He learned to hit other players so hard that after he joined the Bears his blocking would often bring a smile to the usually stern face of "Papa Bear," as Halas was called.

The other Bear linemen were almost as good. The first-string guards were Danny Fortmann and George Musso. The tackles were Joe Stydahar and Lee Artoe. Dick Plasman and George Wilson were the ends. Many of these men played on both offense and defense, since platoon football was still many years away.

The 1940 Bears had no overall personality because the individual players on the team were so varied. Fortmann and Osmanski were serious young men who later became dentists. Plasman, called "Eric the Red," wore no helmet during

games and was known for the violence of his play
and his fiery temperament. George Wilson, the
team's unofficial leader, had the knack of coming
through with the key play. Turner was the most
sociable player. He would often pass the nights
with his banjo, singing out Texas tunes that his
teammates swore would wake the dead. McAfee
and Stydahar, on the other hand, had quiet tem-
peraments.

Off the field, the Bears were a mixed bag of per-
sonalities. On the field, they played as a unit. The
1940 Bears had an element that all great pro teams
have had—teamwork. Although they were players
of varying natures, they all pulled together toward
their ultimate goal, an NFL title.

Chicago opened the 1940 season against the
Green Bay Packers, and it quickly became apparent that Halas' foresight would pay off. The *T*-
formation and Luckman gave the Bears an explosive offense. And George McAfee lighted the fuse.
After the Packers got off to a 3-0 lead on a field
goal, McAfee took the next kickoff and ran 93 yards
for a touchdown. Later, he passed to rookie end
Ken Kavanaugh for a second touchdown, and ran
nine yards for a third score. Luckman, meanwhile,
was preventing the defenses from overloading their
line to stop the Bears' running game. He completed
three of five forward passes for 144 yards. His
longest completion gained 51 yards. (Even with

the *T*-formation, the Bears of 1940 did not pass as often as modern teams.) In all, the balanced Chicago attack gained 333 yards. The Bears won, 41-10. It was a good start.

After resting Monday and Tuesday, the Bears went to Comiskey Park in Chicago on Wednesday night to play their crosstown rivals, the Chicago Cardinals. (In 1940, NFL football schedules were more irregular than they are today.) The Bears were confident of victory and eager to prove how good they were. But they failed to prove anything at all. The Cardinals beat them, 21-7.

But the Bears bounced back, and in the next three games they played like title contenders. In quick succession they beat the Cleveland Browns, 21-14, the Detroit Lions, 7-0, and the Brooklyn (football) Dodgers, 16-7. The *T* was proving to be quite effective, and so was rookie McAfee. After the Brooklyn game, opposing coach Dr. John B. Sutherland called him, "the best back I have seen this year."

The troublesome New York Giants were the next team to make an attempt to stop McAfee. But they concentrated so hard on him that they forgot about another fine rookie, halfback Ray "Scooter" McLean. The little Scooter was playing before a group of rooters from St. Anselm's College of New Hampshire, his alma mater. He didn't let them down. He came off the bench and scored two

*The Bears' Jack Manders kicks a field goal while his
teammates hold off charging New York linemen.*

touchdowns, both of them on passes from Luckman. The Bears won, 37-21.

Luckman's performance was his best of the season up to that point. He completed nine of 14
passes for 171 yards, and he did not stop there. He
also played on defense (as did most players in
those days), knocking down passes in the Bears'
defensive secondary and keeping the opposition
deep in its own territory with his long punts. Luckman was as good—if not better—than the astute
Halas had expected.

A highlight of the New York game was a 52-yard field goal kicked by the Bears' Lee Artoe, who was so near-sighted that he couldn't see the result. In fact, he couldn't even see the goal posts when he kicked the ball. He knew from the impact of his kick that it was close, but he did not know that the ball had gone through the goal posts until he heard Halas shouting, "It's over! It's over!" Then Artoe ran happily off the field.

The Bears' next game was against the Packers, who were much tougher the second time around. Again the Bears needed help from the little man on the bench. This time he was not Scooter McLean but halfback Bobby Swisher of Northwestern. He entered the game in the second half to prevent Green Bay's great end, Don Hutson, from catching passes. Normally, stopping Hutson was difficult enough for two or three players. But Swisher did it by himself, despite great pain. His body was heavily taped to protect two ribs he had broken in an earlier game. Each time he made a tackle, severe pains shot through his body, but Swisher ignored them.

As the game went into its final minutes, Green Bay was trailing, 14-7. Three times the Packers threw for the end zone in an attempt to tie the score. Three times Hutson was there. So was Swisher. He knocked the pass down each time, and the Bears won, 14-7. It did not appear that any

NFL team could stop Halas' fired-up players now.

The following week, in a game with the Detroit Lions, the Bears learned that they weren't invincible. With only 26 seconds remaining, Chicago seemingly had another victory. Luckman had completed seven of nine passes for 167 yards to give the Bears a 14-10 lead. Then Lion quarterback Cotton Price threw a desperation pass to Lloyd Cardwell for a touchdown and a 17-14 upset.

Actually, the key play didn't occur in the last few moments of the game. It had occurred on the second-to-last play in the first half. Chicago halfback Harry Clark had carried the ball to Detroit's one-yard line. There were still 28 seconds left in the quarter, enough time to score a touchdown. At least, that's what the Bears thought.

In their huddle, though, the Bears discovered that Clark was still lying on the ground. An alert Lion had pinned him there illegally after the tackle, and the seconds were ticking away. The sight of Clark struggling to get to his feet aroused Chicago end "Eggs" Manske, who ran over to help Clark. Pulling and tugging at the Lion player, he freed Clark. Although the Lions deserved a penalty for employing such tactics, their attempt to use up time went unnoticed by officials. Instead, the Bears received a 15-yard penalty for unnecessary roughness. To make matters worse, time ran out in the first half.

The Bears had a club rule that placed an automatic fine of $50 on any player who committed a foul in a crucial situation. Manske had merely wanted to see that the vital play was executed before the half ended. Unfortunately, his motives were misunderstood by the officials. The case was exceptional, but Halas was a man who stuck to the rules. He assessed the fine. The other Bears, however, came to Manske's aid. They chipped in and gave the $50 pot to Manske. Even Papa Bear, it was suspected, was a generous contributor.

The Bears tried to forget the disappointing loss and continue their drive to the Western Division title. However, a week later, against Washington, they were again frustrated. With only 40 seconds left in the game, Chicago trailed, 7-3. Substitute quarterback Bob Snyder told McAfee to head for the goal line. "I'll hit you with the ball," he promised. Snyder kept his word. McAfee caught the ball on the Washington 15 and ran to the one for a 49-yard gain before being tackled.

But time was running out. Unless the clock could be stopped, the Bears would lose their opportunity to score. So McAfee faked an injury, which automatically stopped the clock.

This was a trick that Halas' clubs had been using for years. In fact, the Bears had used it so often and so effectively that the NFL had changed the rules. The new rules stated that if a team had only three previous time outs in the half, it could have one more time out in the last two minutes to remove an injured player. If a team had used its four time outs, it could remove an injured player only at the cost of a five-yard penalty.

The Bears, then, were trapped by a rule change they themselves had brought about. They had forgotten that they had used the allotted number of time outs, so they were penalized five yards. That ruled out a rushing situation. The Bears had to pass now and, since it took less time to pass than to run, there might be time for two attempts. Unfortunately, both passes were incomplete.

Halfback Ray Nolting is brought down by Ed Justice of the Washington Redskins. The Bears' last-minute drive failed to score and they lost, 7-3.

The Bears, however, did not accept the loss quietly. After the second pass, which was the final play of the game, the Bears protested that the Redskins' Frank Filchock had interfered with Bear receiver Bill Osmanski. Their angry protest did not change the officials' verdict, however. The Bears lost, 7-3.

The game was over but not forgotten. George Preston Marshall, owner of the Redskins, made sure of that. "They're crybabies," Marshall said, referring to Chicago's protest. "They're front runners. They're not a second-half team. The Bears are quitters."

It was an insult to the Bears, both as players and as men, and they could not forget it easily. Had he known the effect of his words on the Bears, no doubt Marshall would have kept silent. For Chicago swore revenge.

With renewed determination the Bears went into their final two games of the season. They exploded from the *T* to beat Cleveland, 41-25, and the Chicago Cardinals, 31-25. Halas' vision had finally recaptured the Western Division title. Luckman and his teammates had executed on the field what Papa Bear had planned on paper.

To the delight of Chicago, the Washington Redskins were the champions in the Eastern Division. The rematch between the two teams would determine the NFL title. And the Bears would have a chance to make Marshall eat his words. It turned out to be a game that football historians would long remember.

The week before the championship game, the walls of the Bears' clubhouse were covered with clippings reminding them of what Marshall had said after the 7-3 loss.

"I've never experienced anything like it," Luckman would recall later. "There was a feeling of tension in the air, as though something tremendous was about to happen."

Halas, curiously enough, was worried by his team's grimness. "These guys are so mad," he told an assistant, "that they'll be too busy trying to kill the Redskins instead of beating them at football. I've got to calm them down."

Calming them down wasn't easy. Not with George Preston Marshall around. A few days before the game, Marshall said, "The trouble with the league right now is that the strength is concentrated in the East."

The remark made the Bears fume again and the players thought of nothing but revenge. Their state of mind was apparent on the train ride to Washington. In those days ballplayers customarily passed the time on train rides by playing cards or sitting and swapping stories. There was no laughter or joking for the Bears, however. They sat huddled in their seats, and studied their notebooks.

The day before the game, both teams practiced at Griffith Stadium. The Redskins had their workout first. Then came the Bears. By this time, many of the Redskins had showered and were seated in the stands to watch the Western Division champions. What they saw was frightening.

"I got back to the field just as they were coming out," Washington defensive back Andy Farkas recalled later. "They came out screaming like a pack of wild Indians. I'd never seen anything like it. They took off and ran the length of the field. They circled the goal posts and started back, and they were still screaming."

It was an impressive and spontaneous outburst of team spirit. At that moment, Halas turned to his assistant Hunk Anderson and said, "My, but the boys are enthusiastic. Get 'em back inside. I don't want 'em to lose that kind of enthusiasm."

The coach made sure they didn't. "Before the game," Luckman remembered, "Halas did one of the psychologically greatest things I've seen in my life. He never gave us a pep talk. He just told us he had nothing to say. He pointed to the Washington papers and said, 'This is what the people in Washington have to say about you. Gentlemen, we've never been crybabies. Here are the headlines. Go out and play the best football you can.'"

For a second, the room was silent. Then cleats slammed hard onto the concrete floor of the Chicago dressing room, and the Bears stormed onto the playing field. Their pent-up anger was about to explode.

Chicago's game plan was based on a gamble. Halas told Luckman, "I'm taking a chance that the Redskins won't change their defenses. . . . No coach has changed a winning defense."

Although the Bears' strategy was a gamble, it was a good one. This was an era when defenses were limited to a few simple alternatives, rather than the complex maneuvers that two-platoon football uses today. In watching films of the Redskins' game, Halas had discovered that the Bears' most effective plays against Washington were their "counter" plays. In the counter series, Chicago would send a man-in-motion to one side of the field, then run the play in the opposite direction. For example, if one of the Chicago backs was running to the left and the opposing team's secondary was shifting to meet him, then the play would be run to the right, or "against the flow" of the man-in-motion.

Halas had outlined to Luckman three plays to be called the first time the Bears got the ball. He wanted to know immediately if the Redskins were using the same defenses they had used three weeks before, when Chicago had lost, 7-3. If they were, Luckman was to use the counter series.

"On the first play," Halas told Luckman, "I want

COUNTER PLAY

In a typical counter play the quarterback fakes to the halfback, who is moving to the left side (dotted line), then hands off to the fullback. The fake and the use of a split end on the left creates the impression that the play is moving in that direction. The fullback (solid line) fakes a few steps to the left and then runs to the right, or "against the flow" of the man-in-motion (the halfback).

you to send George McAfee inside right tackle. If the defenses are the same, turn Osmanski loose."

So, after Ray Nolting returned the kickoff 22 yards to the 24, Luckman called Halas' play.

Kavanaugh, at left end, went 18 yards out on the flank, and the Washington right halfback followed him out. Nolting, at left half, went in motion to the right, and the Redskin linebacker trailed him out. That was all Luckman needed to know. The first play (an eight-yard gain by McAfee) had shown that Washington's reaction to the man-in-motion *T* was unchanged. The Redskin secondary reacted to the direction of the motion. As a result, the Bears could spread the Redskin defense and then strike at its vulnerable parts.

On the next play, the left end again went wide. Nolting then drove straight ahead into the left side of Washington's line, and Luckman feinted a hand-

Bill Osmanski (9) heads for the Bears' first touchdown of the 1940 championship game.

off to him. Osmanski faked the same way, then turned to the right. Luckman made a reverse pivot and gave the ball to Osmanski, who was running to the spread right side of the Redskin line.

"Bill was really driving when I handed off that ball to him," Luckman said afterwards. "I knew he was going some place in a hurry."

The play, however, did not go as planned. McAfee hadn't made his block properly on the Redskin right end, and Osmanski had to improvise.

"George had him blocked off," Osmanski remembered, "but he was reaching out with his hands, and I was afraid he would grab me, so I just made a sort of dip and went outside around end."

The overshifted linebacker was blocked easily, and suddenly Osmanski was alone with only two Redskins between him and the goal line. The two, Ed Justice and Jimmy Johnston, trapped him near the Washington 35-yard line. But before they could get to him, the Bears' George Wilson, cutting across from his position at right end, hit Johnston with a blind-side block. That sent Johnston sprawling into Justice, and both players went down. To this day, Halas says, "I've never seen a block like it." Osmanski went 68 yards for the touchdown, and Jack Manders added the extra point. The Bears were on their way.

Immediately, Washington tried to even the score. Max Krause took the kickoff and went 62 yards to the Bears' 32-yard line. Then they attempted the scoring play. "Slingin' " Sammy Baugh, the Redskins' great quarterback, faded back and threw a long pass to end Charlie Malone, who was clear of his defenders. Had Malone caught the ball, the result would have been a certain touchdown. And this might have slowed down the fired-up Bears. Fortunately, Malone dropped the ball.

The angry Bears pounced on the missed opportunity, and when they took possession of the ball, they scored again. And they did so by simply running over the Redskins. They moved the ball 80 yards in 17 plays without throwing a pass. Luckman scored on a sneak play from the one-foot line. Washington appeared baffled. They had limited the Bears to a mere field goal in their previous game. But now Chicago was driving right through them. The Bears were not the same team.

Still, Washington did not quit. They immediately tried to get back into the game. That meant Baugh had to pass the ball. Three times he threw, and three times Chicago defenders knocked the ball down. The Bears' defense was just as determined as the offense. It did not seem as if Washington had a chance.

Chicago confirmed the hopelessness of Washington's plight on the very next play. With the ball at the Washington 42, Luckman called for almost the same play that had worked for the first touchdown by Osmanski. This time, Joe Maniaci was the fullback. He went 42 yards for the third touchdown, and Phil Martinovich added the extra point. The score was 21-0, and the Bears were not yet finished for the first half.

They scored once more. Luckman threw a 30-yard pass to Kavanaugh in the end zone. Kavanaugh leaped behind Filchock and Farkas and caught the ball for a touchdown. Snyder converted to make the score, 28-0, at the half.

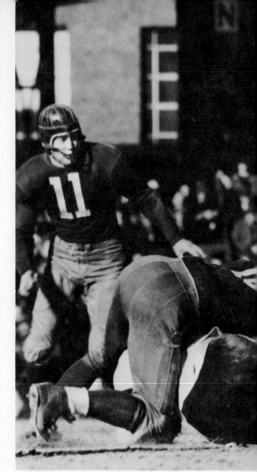

George McAfee near-ly loses his balance as he weaves through Redskin tacklers.

The 36,034 Washington fans sat in stunned disbelief. The Redskins had entered the game with a better record, and they were favored to win. But Washington had not reckoned on the fury of the Bears. Chicago was making Marshall pay for his taunting criticism. And in the Chicago dressing room, Halas was not letting his team forget. He reminded the Bears that they had been called a "first-half ballclub" and "quitters." Ordinarily, with a 28-point lead, they might have eased up in

the second half. Instead Halas urged the Bears to pour it on, and they returned to the field with renewed anger.

On the second play of the third period, Baugh tried a short pass to Johnston, but Chicago defensive end Hampton Pool anticipated the play. He batted the ball into the air, caught it and ran 15 yards for the touchdown.

That finished the Redskins. The Bears scored three more times in the third period. They could not be stopped. First, Nolting ran 23 yards through left tackle for a touchdown. Then George McAfee intercepted a pass thrown by reserve quarterback Roy Zimmerman of Washington, and went 34 yards for another score. And the Bears kept driving. Even "Bulldog" Turner got into the act. The big lineman intercepted another Zimmerman pass and ran 21 yards to score.

The "first-half ballclub" didn't stop in the fourth quarter, either. Anger still spurred the Bears on. Harry Clark ran 44 yards for a touchdown. Gary Famiglietti scored from the two-yard line. Then Clark scored again, this time from the one. There had never been anything like this game in NFL history.

During the fourth quarter, the public-address man chose to tell the Washington crowd: "Those who wish to purchase season tickets for next year . . ." His ill-timed announcement was drowned out by the boos.

After the Bears had scored their 11th touchdown, referee Red Friesell jogged over to Halas on the sidelines with a problem.

"George," he said, "I'm in a terrible jam. The fans have kept every football kicked into the stands after each conversion. This is the last football we have. Would you mind asking your boys not to kick for the extra point, but to run or pass for it?"

Halas was happy to oblige. The Bears passed

After beating the Redskins, 73-0, the jubilant Bears cheer Coach Halas.

for the extra point.

The final score was 73-0, the most one-sided result for a championship game in the history of the NFL. The Bears had dominated the game from the first series of downs. They had played with maniacal devotion to total victory. Even late in the fourth quarter, players leaving the field had urged their replacements: "Pour it on 'em. Don't let up. Pour it on."

Their courage as a football team had been questioned, and the Bears had answered in the best possible way. By winning convincingly, they had silenced the insults forever. It was a fitting revenge.

The Redskins were not completely shamed that afternoon, though. They deserve credit for their persistence. They battled down to the end, but the Bears simply overpowered them. For the majority of the Redskins, it was the most frustrating experience of their lives. Wee Willie Wilkin, their blond tackle, had to be led off the field late in the game, crying in anger and shame.

When the Redskins' humiliation ended with the sound of the gun, a newsman turned to his colleagues in the press box and quipped, "Marshall just shot himself." Marshall would have had good reason. His remarks had lit the fire in the Bears that had destroyed his team. His words had come back to haunt him.

And the Bears still remembered those words. In the Chicago dressing room, they reminded each other of what they had been playing for that afternoon.

"Not bad for a team of quitters," a voice boomed from the showers.

"Not bad at all," Halas shouted back. "Not bad at all."

And in the glum Washington quarters, reporters were asking quarterback Sammy Baugh if the game would have been different had Malone caught the "sure" touchdown pass early in the game.

Sammy thought for a moment and then, with a poker face, answered, "Yes, the score would have been 73-7."

LOS ANGELES RAMS
1951

After Joe Stydahar became the coach of the Los Angeles Rams in 1950, he seemed to age more quickly than most people. His hair turned gray; he couldn't sleep; he was in and out of medical clinics for intestinal trouble brought on by emotional disturbance. "What Joe needs," said the Rams' physician at the end of the 1950 season, "is a long rest."

The cause of Stydahar's condition was his team. Although the Rams were immensely talented, they were also an erratic team. On good days, they were unstoppable. In 1950, they had beaten Baltimore, 70-27; Detroit, 65-24; Green Bay, 45-14 and 51-14. Unfortunately, Los Angeles did not always play hard enough to produce many good days.

In Stydahar's first year, for instance, the Rams

lost two of their first four games. In one of these games the Philadelphia Eagles beat them, 56-20. Stydahar fumed over the Rams' poor performances. He thought they were not hitting as hard as they should on the playing field. After the fiasco with the Eagles, Stydahar decided to straighten the team out.

The Rams' dressing room was silent when the coach entered. It did not remain so for long. The 284-pound Stydahar launched into a noisy speech. He strode up and down the room hurling insults and challenges, working himself into a rage. Then he did something that no Ram player ever forgot: he reached into his mouth and extracted a denture from where his front teeth should have been. As a lineman for the Chicago Bears 15 years earlier, Stydahar had lost his teeth in a game against Detroit. Now he brandished the false teeth and shouted, "That's why you can't win! You've all got your own teeth! Nobody has the guts to charge in with his head up."

"Big Joe" was not finished. Before leaving the room, he warned the Rams: "From now on, I want to see some teeth and blood flying or there'll be some changes made."

The Los Angeles players responded to Stydahar's crackdown by playing harder. As a result, they won seven of their last eight games, plus the National Conference championship. (Until 1949

The Rams and the Browns watch intently as Lou Groza's kick sails between the uprights to win the 1950 championship game.

NFL teams were divided into Eastern and Western divisions. From 1950-1952 the league was broken up into American and National Conference divisions. Since 1953 the NFL has been divided into the Eastern Conference and the Western Conference.) Stydahar hoped to conclude the season by winning the NFL championship game. Unfortunately, Los Angeles lost to the Cleveland Browns, 30-27, when Lou Groza kicked a 16-yard field goal with only 28 seconds remaining. It was the second year in a row that the Rams had failed to win the title game. In 1949 they had lost to the Philadelphia Eagles, 14-0. Many people began to think of Los Angeles as merely a flashy team that couldn't win under the pressure of a championship game.

Stydahar thought differently. He considered Los Angeles a potential champion. So did the players. They had expected to beat the Browns, and after the loss many of them sat in front of their lockers and wept. When Stydahar saw how disappointed they were, he himself was moved to tears. That afternoon, Stydahar and the Rams began looking forward to the next season, when they would have another chance to prove they could win the big game.

When the 1951 season finally opened, Stydahar realized that winning the NFL title would be no easy task. For one thing, he had lost so many veteran players from the previous year's team—including every veteran tackle—that he was forced to keep 12 rookies on his roster. This was more than any other contender in the NFL had. Some of the rookies—for example, Andy Robustelli of little Arnold College and Norb Hecker from Baldwin-Wallace College—seemed quite promising. But Stydahar knew that rookies are more likely to make mistakes in a game; and he also knew that championship teams cannot afford mistakes.

A bigger problem for Stydahar was what to do with Bob Waterfield and Norm Van Brocklin, his two quarterbacks. Both were brilliant field generals and, in 1950, Stydahar had used them alternately in each game. Neither Waterfield nor Van Brocklin had liked his part-time role, but the strategy had been successful. The 1950 Rams had broken nearly every offensive record in the league. They had gained 5,420 yards, 3,709 by passing. They had made 278 first downs and had completed 253 passes, 31 for touchdowns. They had scored 466 points, 70 of which were scored in a game against Baltimore. In one quarter of a game against Detroit, they had scored 41 points.

The results justified Stydahar's strategy, but Big Joe knew that there was always a chance that his plans might backfire in 1951. If Waterfield and Van Brocklin became disenchanted with sharing the job, their performances might suffer. And without the all-important passing attacks of the two quarterbacks, the Rams would be lost.

In spite of this possibility, Stydahar was determined to gamble on a two-quarterback system. His reasoning was based on the fierce competition that existed between the two men. In every game they would try to outdo each other. Stydahar felt that if Waterfield and Van Brocklin could maintain a healthy rivalry, they would lead the Rams to an NFL championship.

However, the coach had to handle the situation delicately. Already Los Angeles fans were split into Waterfield and Van Brocklin factions. Stydahar could not permit this sort of dissension to spread to the team itself. It was a difficult problem which required a great deal of tact, for no two men were more dissimilar than Waterfield and Van Brocklin.

Waterfield was an all-round player: he ran, passed and also punted and place-kicked. In 1949, when Van Brocklin was a rookie substitute quarterback, Waterfield had led the Rams to the division title; he had completed 154 of 296 passes for 2,168 yards, and led the league with nine field goals. As a result of his performance that year, he was named All-Pro quarterback for the third time in his career. In 1950, Waterfield was injured early in the season. When he finally recovered, he found himself sharing the quarterback job with Van

Brocklin, who had filled in quite capably in his absence. But Waterfield was responsible for leading the Rams to the conference title in 1950. In the conference play-off against the Chicago Bears, he threw three touchdown passes to end Tom Fears and kicked a field goal in a 24-14 victory.

Although he caused a great deal of excitement on the football field, Waterfield was really a reserved individual. He was married to movie star Jane Russell, his sweetheart from his days at Van Nuys (California) High School, but he did not care for crowds and parties. He was a loner who enjoyed life most when he was with a few old friends or by himself, hunting and fishing.

Van Brocklin, on the other hand, was an entirely different sort of person. As a player, he lacked most of Waterfield's natural skills. In fact, all he really could do was pass the ball. But that was enough for Stydahar, who thought that throwers like Van Brocklin could win NFL titles. To other people in the league, Van Brocklin was something of an oddity. A coach with the San Francisco 49ers said: "If the game hadn't turned pass-happy, Van Brocklin wouldn't be able to play even with the semipros. All he has is an arm. He runs like a girl with her girdle slipping. He couldn't block a baby or play any other position. Just blow hard and he falls down."

Wise old George Halas agreed. "Van Brocklin

can throw—period!" he said. "In the full sense of the word, he is not a professional player."

Van Brocklin himself didn't care what people said about him. He was concerned only with winning football games, and he did this the best way he knew how—by throwing the football. In 1949, his rookie year, he did not play much at first. But over the season Van Brocklin showed the Rams that he had the potential to be an NFL quarterback. In the last game of the season, which Los Angeles had to win to stay alive in the race for the division title, Van Brocklin was given a chance to play. He threw four touchdown passes and led the Rams to a 52-27 victory.

In 1950 Van Brocklin played more often. In fact, he won the NFL passing title by completing 127 of 233 passes for 2,061 yards and 18 touchdowns. During that time, the Rams found him an intense competitor. Every time Los Angeles lost a game, whether or not he had anything to do with it, Van Brocklin went into a rage. Often, after a loss, he would bang his fists on the clubhouse walls, sob uncontrollably and kick anything handy. Later he would keep his wife up all night by drinking black coffee, cracking his knuckles and muttering, "We should'a won, we should'a won." In contrast, Waterfield was able to keep his emotions in check.

Waterfield and Van Brocklin were not, however, Stydahar's only problems. Big Joe had only to re-

call the Rams' 56-20 loss to the Eagles the year before to know that football players sometimes grow
too satisfied. He swore not to allow that to happen
to the Rams during the 1951 season, even if he
aged in the process. However, it wasn't long before the players became complacent again, forcing
Stydahar to use harsh measures to maintain discipline.

It happened after the Rams beat the Eagles in
an exhibition game in Little Rock, Arkansas. Afterwards, the Rams went out to celebrate, and the
celebration went so well that most of the players
abused Stydahar's team curfew. By 2 A.M.—curfew time—most of them had not returned to their
hotel rooms. So Stydahar called several night clubs
in Little Rock until he got Jack Finlay, one of the
Rams' veteran guards.

Pretending he was a player, Stydahar asked Finlay if any of the other Rams were there.

"Sure," said Jack, laughing. "We're all here.
Come on."

Stydahar roared into the phone, "Listen, this is
Stydahar! You guys have thirty minutes to get to
the hotel. And you're fined a hundred bucks each.
And another hundred if it takes you longer than
thirty minutes to get here!"

Stydahar fined the Rams a total of $7,400, a
league record, but he later refunded the money
when they proved they could be serious about

football. The players *were* serious. They knew
they had a reputation as a team that crumbled under pressure, and they wanted to prove their ability to win the NFL championship. And on paper,
at least, the Rams appeared able to do so.

To distract opposing teams and prevent them
from overwhelming Waterfield or Van Brocklin,
the Rams had a number of talented running backs
they could turn loose. For pure speed, Los Angeles
had the following players: pigeon-toed Verda
Thomas Smith, better known as "Vitamin T.;" little Tommy Kalmanir (5 feet 8½ inches, 170
pounds); and Glenn Davis, who had been one-half
of the famous Davis-Blanchard duo at West Point.

Representing power, there were: Dick Hoerner
(6 feet 4 inches, 220 pounds); Dan Towler (6
feet 2 inches, 220 pounds), called "Deacon" because he was a divinity student; and Paul "Tank"
Younger (6 feet 4 inches, 226 pounds), who had
been used primarily on defense in 1950. Before the
season began, Stydahar thought of using Younger
more frequently as a ball carrier, but decided
against it. He would reconsider later on.

Although Waterfield and Van Brocklin received
considerable support from the running backs, their
most indispensable teammates were pass-catching
ends Tom Fears and Elroy "Crazylegs" Hirsch.
The veteran Fears had led the league in receptions
for three straight years—from 1948 to 1950.

Hirsch was a newcomer as a pass receiver, having been a halfback when Stydahar became coach in 1950. But Big Joe had taken one look at the way Elroy could change directions so sharply and had converted him to a split end. It was a smart move because in 1950 Hirsch caught 42 passes for 687 yards and seven touchdowns.

In the opening game against the New York Yankees (who later became the Dallas Texans and, eventually, the Baltimore Colts), the defending National Conference champs showed the rest of the NFL the sort of competition they could expect that season. The Rams beat the Yanks, 54-14.

In that contest Van Brocklin completed 27 of 41 passes for five touchdowns and 554 yards, breaking an NFL record for most yards gained on passes in one game. Three of his touchdown passes were caught by Hirsch. During the game Waterfield sat on the bench with an injury.

The Rams' next game was against Cleveland, and Waterfield had recovered in time to play. With both men healthy, Stydahar went back to his two-quarterback system. Many observers were surprised by this because they felt that Van Brocklin deserved to play the whole game on the basis of his performance against the Yankees. It didn't really matter. Neither Van Brocklin (six completions of 17 passes) nor Waterfield (six of 16) could hit his receivers. Cleveland won, 38-23.

For the experts, the game proved the Browns' championship victory over the Rams had been no fluke. For Los Angeles fans, it proved only that Stydahar's two-quarterback system had to go; they booed the Rams' coach mercilessly. Stydahar was in a difficult position. He seemed to age more with each defeat. But Big Joe stuck to his original decision. He continued alternating Waterfield and Van Brocklin.

In the next two games both quarterbacks improved and Los Angeles beat Detroit, 27-21, and Green Bay, 28-0. This quieted Stydahar's critics, but not for long. They were highly vocal after San Francisco upset the Rams, 44-17, the following week. Once again, Van Brocklin (13 completions of 30 passes) and Waterfield (seven of 16) could not move the team. And, once again, the fans blamed Stydahar.

But Stydahar had less responsibility for the defeat than did the crafty 49er coach, Buck Shaw. While plotting his strategy before the game, he had realized that San Francisco would be helpless unless it could contain the Rams' passing attack. Shaw found a unique way to solve the 49ers' problem. He replaced his hefty, slow-footed linebackers—Norm Standlee and Don Burke—with the quick, smaller-sized halfbacks, Verl Lillywhite and Jim Powers. It was an unheard-of move because, traditionally, linebackers must be quite

Jim Winkler, a 248-pound Ram tackle, brings down the 185-pound Lillywhite in the Rams' second meeting with the 49ers. Los Angeles won, 23-13.

large in order to stop hard-moving backs. Shaw wasn't particularly concerned with the Rams' rushing game. He was hoping to neutralize the speed of pass receivers Fears and Hirsch by using Lillywhite and Powers. Since the two 49er backs could match the Rams' ends step-for-step, Shaw's plan was successful.

Strangely enough, Los Angeles' next game was also played against the 49ers. This time, however, Stydahar had a remedy for Shaw's unusual defense. The Rams' coach used three fullbacks on offense to overpower the 5-foot 10-inch, 185-pound

Lillywhite and the 6-foot, 185-pound Powers. To put together this combination Stydahar switched Tank Younger from the defensive squad and teamed him with Towler and Hoerner in the backfield. The concentration of Ram power was too much for Lillywhite and Powers, who were just too small to stop the trio. San Francisco coach Shaw was forced to send his big boys—Standlee and Burke—back to their linebacker spots. When he did, Stydahar countered by bringing in his speedy running backs—Glenn Davis and Vitamin Smith.

The combination of speed and power worked— the Rams gained 159 yards on the ground. Meanwhile, Waterfield picked the defenses apart with his passing, completing 11 of 22 passes for 188 yards. This time Los Angeles won, 23-13.

From the victory, Stydahar discovered how effective Towler, Hoerner and Younger could be together. Now no team could afford to sacrifice strength for speed to cope with Los Angeles' tricky ends, Hirsch and Fears. All Stydahar had to do was to summon his power backs, known as the "Bull Elephants." After the victory over the 49ers, Stydahar employed the Bull Elephants regularly. They had developed from an emergency measure into a powerful offensive weapon.

The Rams won their next two games against the Chicago Cardinals, 45-21, and the Yankees again,

48-21. In both games, the new Bull Elephant back-field, with its jackrabbit counterpart (Davis, Smith and Kalmanir), made life miserable for the de-fense. Against the Yankees, the running game was especially effective. Towler gained 150 yards; Hoerner, 78; Smith, 62; Davis, 33; and Younger, 32. In all, Los Angeles made 366 yards on the ground.

It seemed that no one could stop the Rams now. But the very next week the Washington Redskins beat them, 31-21, and they did so by holding the Los Angeles ground attack to 61 yards. The Red-skins simply outhit the Rams all afternoon, a fact that did not escape Stydahar's attention. "Disgust-ing," he told the Rams afterwards. "You looked like a bunch of old ladies out there."

The Rams certainly did not play like old ladies the next week against the Chicago Bears. Behind, 14-0, in a game they could not afford to lose, they fought to overcome the lead. With the ball on the Rams' own nine-yard line, Waterfield called a favorite pass play, one 'hat developed from a standard run. The Bears were fooled, and Water-field hit Hirsch with a pass in the open. Crazylegs, who had replaced Fears as the NFL's top re-ceiver, caught the ball and ran 91 yards for the touchdown.

It was the break Los Angeles needed. Now the Bull Elephants went to work. Four times they

The speedy "Vitamin" Smith carries the ball as

Dick Hoerner prepares to block a Yankee tackler.

drove 80 yards or more downfield for the touchdown. Then one of Stydahar's dozen rookies, Andy
Robustelli, blocked a Chicago punt for still another Los Angeles touchdown. The final score was
42-17. To Ram fans the team seemed to be on the
right track again.

But the following week, in their unpredictable
fashion, the Rams lost to previously conquered
Detroit, 24-22, giving Stydahar still another week
of sleepless nights. The defeat also gave Stydahar
little chance of guiding the Rams to a championship. As Los Angeles went into its final game
against Green Bay, it was tied for second place
with the Chicago Bears, half a game behind the
Detroit Lions. The Rams would win the championship only if they beat the Packers and if the Lions
and Bears both lost.

Los Angeles took care of the Packers by beating
them, 42-14. Waterfield threw five touchdown
passes. Hirsch made three touchdown catches
and finished the season as the league's leading receiver with 66 pass receptions for 1,495 yards and
17 touchdowns. But the most exciting news concerned what had happened elsewhere. It was the
answer to the Rams' prayers—the Lions had lost
to the 49ers and the Bears had lost to the Cardinals. The Rams were the champions of the National Conference. In the locker room afterwards,
the players were jubilant.

So was Stydahar. But even in a moment of triumph, he had headaches—he and Van Brocklin were holding a grudge against one another. The ill will had developed during the Packer game, when the coach had sent in a running play. Van Brocklin—as he sometimes did—shook the play off and threw an unsuccessful pass. Annoyed, Stydahar benched him for the rest of the game. Van Brocklin resented his treatment. After the game, he made a statement against Stydahar to newspaper reporters: "I'd just as soon play somewhere else next year than play for that man," he said.

The statement served only to inflame Big Joe's anger. He made plans to keep "The Dutchman," as Van Brocklin was called, on the bench in the championship game against the Cleveland Browns.

While Van Brocklin was fuming, the other players prepared to meet the Browns. That was a chore large enough for any team. In only their second season in the league, the Browns had won 11 straight games, after losing their opener to San Francisco. A Cleveland dynasty appeared to be in the making. Few people gave Los Angeles much of a chance against the defending NFL champs.

The most obvious reason the Rams were underdogs was their record of two losses in championship games. The players knew that they had a reputation for losing under pressure and they wanted to prove that it was undeserved.

All during the week, the Rams grimly prepared for the game. Grimmest of all was Van Brocklin. He and Stydahar scarcely spoke to each other. The Dutchman was still incensed about being benched in the Packer game. Big Joe was just as angry. He could not forgive Van Brocklin for airing the grudge in public. Had The Dutchman kept silent, Stydahar, more than likely, would have treated the incident as just another case of Van Brocklin's fiery nature. As it stood, Stydahar could not forgive him.

Not surprisingly, then, the moody quarterback was sitting on the bench when the championship game started, and he stayed there all through the scoreless first quarter. The roar of 59,500 fans in the Los Angeles Coliseum, the largest crowd ever to attend a pro game up to that time, stirred Van Brocklin's competitive blood, but it didn't matter to Stydahar. He was sticking with Waterfield. So Van Brocklin cracked his knuckles and muttered on through the second quarter about having the bad luck to play for an ogre like Big Joe.

Early in the second quarter, Waterfield put more energy into the Rams' attack. Los Angeles was on its own 49-yard line, third down and six yards to go for a first down. Waterfield threw a pass to Vitamin T. Smith for a first down at the 33. Three plays later, he threw to Smith again. This time the officials ruled that the Browns had inter-

fered with Smith as he tried to catch the ball. The
penalty gave the Rams a first down at the Cleveland 12, the point where the interference had occurred. Now Waterfield switched to his running
game. Hoerner went through right tackle to the
Cleveland eight. Then Smith drove to the seven.
The Rams were picking up momentum. Towler
carried the ball around right end for six yards and
a first down to the one. From that point, the Rams
didn't waste any time. On first down, Hoerner
smashed through for the touchdown. After Waterfield kicked the extra point the score was 7-0.

*Ram quarterback Bob Waterfield is flipped into the
air by a Cleveland tackler during the 1951 championship game.*

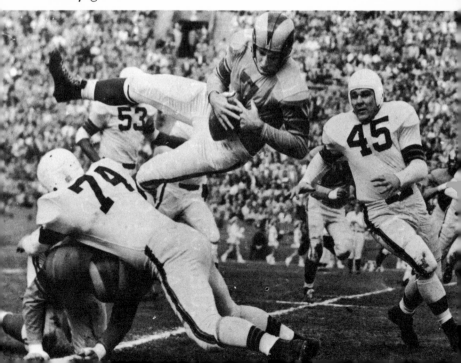

The lead did not last long, however. With three minutes and seven seconds left in the second quarter, the Browns' Lou Groza kicked a 52-yard field goal. The score was now 7-3. The kick was a playoff record for the longest field goal, exceeding the previous record by 10 yards. Less than two minutes later, Cleveland took the lead when Otto Graham completed three consecutive passes for a total gain of 54 yards. The last pass went to Dub Jones for 17 yards and the touchdown. At halftime the Browns led, 10-7, and the experts were nodding their heads knowingly.

Cleveland had the momentum now, but Los Angeles was certainly not going to concede the game. Twice in the past, the Rams had come close to achieving their goal of an NFL championship. The fact that they trailed by three points didn't bother them. Another half of playing time remained—enough for anything to happen.

On the bench The Dutchman was hoping the situation would give him a chance to play, but he thought it was unlikely. Stydahar had not even glanced in his direction during the first half.

When Stydahar ordered his team onto the field for the second half, the Rams smacked their hands together and shouted, "All right, let's get 'em."

The first time Cleveland had the ball, the Los Angeles defense put heavy pressure on Brown quarterback Otto Graham. Defensive end Larry

"Deacon" Dan Towler makes a ten-yard gain as Elroy Hirsch blocks out a Cleveland tackler.

Brink broke through the Browns' line, chased and finally caught Graham. He hit him so hard that Graham fumbled. The alert Robustelli, breaking through from the other end, scooped up the ball at the Browns' 24 and lumbered with it to the Cleveland two. It was the kind of play that discredits football theories about the inadequacies of rookies. Starting two yards from the goal line, Towler made three successive attempts to score. The third time Deacon Dan muscled his way through right guard for the touchdown. After adding the extra point Los Angeles pulled ahead by a score of 14-10.

The Rams kept up the pressure. Early in the fourth quarter, defensive back Marv Johnson intercepted a pass from Graham on the Cleveland 36-yard line and ran all the way to the Browns' one.

Then a strange thing happened. Stydahar looked down the bench to Van Brocklin. "Van," he barked, "get in there and get us a touchdown."

Van Brocklin blinked, then realized that the coach had called for him. As The Dutchman got to his feet, the Los Angeles crowd cheered. Van Brocklin ran onto the field, determined to lead the Rams to a touchdown.

On the third down, with two feet to go for the score, Ram linemen Charley Toogood and Stan West opened a big hole for a quarterback sneak.

"Crazy-Legs" Hirsch reaches out to snare a pass during the championship game.

But Van Brocklin was so jittery that he started before the ball was snapped. The "in-motion" penalty set the Rams back to the Cleveland six. They had to settle for a field goal by Waterfield. Los Angeles 17, Cleveland 10.

Coming off the field, Van Brocklin heard boos this time. He knew he deserved them. His error was inexcusable. He did not even glance at Stydahar as he found his place on the bench and angrily ripped his helmet off. Even his teammates could not soothe him.

Van Brocklin's error became even more important when Cleveland tied the score at 17-17 on a 70-yard drive late in the quarter. The Dutchman scowled at the scoreboard and hoped that Stydahar would give him another chance. Fortunately, Big Joe sensed that Van Brocklin would make people forget his mistake. "Van," he called out, "let's get us the winner."

Van Brocklin was too embarrassed to look at his coach. He was so grateful for another chance that even the boos that greeted his appearance did not bother him. With little more than seven-and-a-half minutes remaining in the game, Van Brocklin took over.

He soon made Stydahar seem like a prophet. On the second down, with three yards to go, at the Los Angeles 27, Van Brocklin sent Fears straight downfield. The veteran end, covered by Brown

Coach Stydahar and the Rams celebrate their 24-17 victory.

safetymen Tommy James and Cliff Lewis, found a way to slide between them. And while Fears was maneuvering, Van Brocklin was coolly waiting. When he saw Fears make his move, The Dutchman threw the ball. Fears caught it a step behind the defenders and went 73 yards for the touchdown. The crowd went wild. As Van Brocklin trotted off the field, he received a standing ovation. The Dutchman had more than atoned for his earlier error. More important, he had helped his Ram teammates prove that they could stand up under the pressure of a championship game.

Minutes later, another of Stydahar's rookies, defensive back Norb Hecker, broke up a short fourth-down pass to end the Browns' last drive. The Los Angeles Rams were the new champions of the NFL. The final score was 24-17.

In the Rams' dressing room, Stydahar and Van Brocklin were shaking hands and telling each other that all was forgiven. The players were laughing and shouting. Flash bulbs blinked everywhere. Champagne corks were popping. It was a celebration that had been three years in the making.

"Any curfew on this one, coach?" the Rams asked jokingly.

"I'll fine you," Stydahar quipped, "if you *don't* have a good time."

The Rams followed the boss's instructions.

A short while later, Stydahar checked into the Scripps Clinic at LaJolla, California, for a complete physical. He had had a strenuous season, a fact that the checkup confirmed. "This patient," the doctors reported in classic understatement, "is laboring under marked mental tension." The doctors prescribed plenty of rest. This time Big Joe didn't mind. He had earned it.

NEW YORK GIANTS
1956

On the day after the 1953 season ended, New York Giant assistant coach Jim Lee Howell prepared to leave his rented apartment on Staten Island in New York for his 700-acre ranch in Arkansas. There was, however, one chore left to be done. Giant owner Wellington Mara had asked him to stop by the team's office before he headed south.

When Howell double-parked his car on a busy Manhattan street, he expected to be only a minute. He stayed considerably longer than that. For 17 floors up, in the Giants' office, Mara was saying that he'd like Howell to be the new coach of the team. Howell was stunned. Although he knew the job was open, he had not even suspected that the Giants would offer him the position. But he did not take long to decide what to do. Yes, he told

Mara, he would be pleased to be coach of the New York Giants.

Then, in a daze, he went down to his car. At first, he didn't notice that a policeman was writing a ticket for double parking. When he finally saw the officer, he explained, "I only thought I'd be gone for a few minutes. I never thought I'd be gone this long. I never thought they'd make me coach."

"Coach?" said the policeman. "Coach of what?"

"The Giants," said Howell. "You know, the football team."

The policeman shook his head and returned the pen and ticket to his pocket. "Coach of the Giants?" he said, with a mocking smile. "Mister, you've got enough troubles without this. You need all the breaks you can get."

Howell did indeed have trouble. The previous New York coach, Steve Owen, had fallen behind the times in football strategy. The modern emphasis was on attack, but defense was Owen's favorite subject. During the late 1940s Owen had created the "umbrella defense," which used a loose semicircle of defenders in the backfield to effectively break up or intercept passes.

Offensively, the Giants were not as up to date, however. They had adjusted easily to the new T-formation when it was introduced in the pros, but once Cleveland coach Paul Brown began to revolutionize the game with his pass patterns in the early 1950s, the Giants became outdated. In 1953, after the Giants had won only three games and had lost nine, Owen resigned.

After taking over, Howell immediately set about to rebuild the Giants. First he talked quarterback Charlie Conerly out of retiring. For several seasons, Conerly had been rushed relentlessly by opponents and he had developed a reputation for not being able to get his passes off in time. Whenever the Giants lost, which was often, Conerly was booed without pity by New York fans. The truth of the matter was that he never received the necessary protection from his blockers.

The 1953 season had been particularly disastrous for Conerly. By midseason, fans were hanging signs from the upper deck and bleachers of New York's Polo Grounds reading, CHARLIE MUST GO.

Conerly became so unpopular that he generally stayed in his hotel room after workouts. On one of the rare evenings he did go out, he and his wife, plus other Giants and their wives, went to the old Madison Square Garden for a hockey game. At one point, the football players were introduced to the crowd and a fan started cursing Conerly.

"Let me handle this, Charlie," a burly lineman said. Then, pointing at the fan, he shouted, "Hey, you up there . . ."

The fan took one look at the lineman and departed in haste.

"We ought to catch that fellow and sign him up," said tackle Bill Austin, referring to the man's speed in leaving.

"Yeah," said another Giant, "but who can catch him?"

Even though Conerly had no admirers in the gallery of Madison Square Garden he had one in his new coach. Howell felt that Conerly would be more than adequate once the Giants straightened out their offense. With the aid of Assistant Coach Vince Lombardi, Howell managed to give Conerly some help. His first step was the conversion of defensive back Frank Gifford to offensive halfback.

Gifford was a handsome young man who had played tailback at the University of Southern California, where he had demonstrated his ability to run and throw the ball well. Howell and Lombardi envisioned him as a kind of multiple-threat halfback. On pitchout plays, Gifford would be able to run or pass. With the ability to do either, he would be able to exploit hesitant defenses.

Howell also added deception to the New York attack. During the spring of 1954, he had visited Clemson College's coach, Frank Howard. Howell had come away impressed by Howard's use of *conversions,* a system by which the quarterback could change plays at the line of scrimmage. This enabled the quarterback to take advantage of weaknesses he might detect in the defense. The *conversions* were the forerunner of the *audibles, checkoffs* and *automatics* that the pros use today.

But New York needed more than deception to improve its performance. Howell still had the problem of providing his quarterback with pass protection, so the coach started to obtain the necessary players. On the offensive line, he already had a potentially good blocking corps in second-year linemen Roosevelt Brown, Jack Stroud and Ray Wietecha and veterans Bill Austin and Dick Yelvington. But he strengthened the Giants' blocking by adding ends Bob Schnelker and Ken MacAfee.

With Schnelker, MacAfee and Kyle Rote, the Giants now had a fine trio of receivers for Conerly. For reserve quarterback, Howell obtained Don Heinrich in the college draft. During the next couple of seasons, Howell would often begin a game with Heinrich, who was a ball-control quarterback. Heinrich would maintain possession of the ball by moving it on the ground with consistent, short-yardage plays. This strategy was intended to limit the chances of the other team to take possession of the ball and also to wear down the defenses for Conerly, who could then pass more successfully.

Although New York possessed a strong defense,

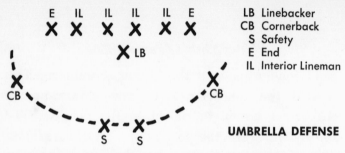

LB	Linebacker
CB	Cornerback
S	Safety
E	End
IL	Interior Lineman

UMBRELLA DEFENSE

In an early version of Steve Owen's umbrella defense, the backs played close to the line of scrimmage to stop rushes. But as opposing teams added more passing to their attacks, the Giants' defense had to adjust. So Owen moved the defensive backs farther from the line, creating a loose semicircle of defenders in the backfield to break up or intercept passes. The arrangement of the players (six interior linemen, one linebacker and four backs) explains why the formation was known as a "6-1-4" defense.

there was still room for improvement. Assistant coach Tom Landry took Owen's umbrella concept and carried it even farther. Originally, to protect against a pass, the ends on a six-man line would drop back and the defensive backs would move farther from the line of scrimmage. This was known as a "6-1-4" defense. Landry switched to a "4-3-4" arrangement, in which there were four interior linemen, three linebackers and four defensive backs. (This is the basic defensive arrangement of today's teams, but more intricate maneuvers have been added since Landry's time.) To strengthen these defenses, New York obtained halfback Dick Nolan in the college draft, traded for linebacker Bill Svoboda and got linebacker Cliff Livingston from the military.

The new players and the improved tactics were a big help. In Howell's first year, the Giants won seven games and lost five, finishing in third place.

Although the fans booed Conerly occasionally, it was obvious that the Giants were making progress.

At the end of the 1954 season, Howell sought to make the Giants even stronger by drafting fullback Mel Triplett, defensive back Jim Patton and defensive tackle Roosevelt Grier. In trades, the Giants obtained defensive end Walt Yowarsky and linebacker Harland Svare. From the Canadian League came Alex Webster, a 6-foot 3-inch, 215-pound running back. Webster had been cut by the Washington Redskins before turning to Canadian football, where he had starred. He was determined to prove that he belonged in the NFL.

With the additional talent, Howell expected to improve on the previous season. But the Giants did not start well, losing four of their first five games. Howell offered his resignation, but it was refused. The Giants split their next two games, routing Washington and then losing to Cleveland. The team was stumbling.

At this point, assistant coaches Lombardi and Ed Kolman came up with the idea of incorporating *T*-formation rushing with single-wing blocking. "Everyone is brush-blocking with the *T* these days," said Lombardi. By this he meant that the offensive linemen were just nudging the defense enough for the runner to get by or so that a subsequent blocker would have a better blocking angle. All blocking was strictly one-on-one. "Ed and

I thought," continued Lombardi, "that if we put double-team blocking [two blockers hitting one defender] into our running game, we'd catch a lot of teams by surprise. I don't think there's a lineman in the game today who can handle a double-team block."

Howell liked the idea and set to work right away. He designed two running plays to make use of double-team blocking. In one of them Gifford would head for a hole opened between tackle and end. In the other Webster would head for the same spot on the other side of the line. After drilling the Giants in the new plays, Howell turned his club loose. The new tactic worked. The Giants won four of their last five games and moved from last place to third in the East with a record of six wins, five losses and one tie. Their brilliant finish was a promise of things to come.

At the end of the season, Howell continued to strengthen New York. He drafted linebacker Sam Huff, defensive end Jim Katcavage and punter Don Chandler. In trades New York fared even better, picking up defensive tackle Dick "Little Mo" Modzelewski, defensive end Andy Robustelli and halfbacks Gene Filipski and Ed Hughes. The deal for Robustelli came about unexpectedly. At the time Robustelli's wife was about to have a baby, and he asked his team, the Los Angeles Rams, if he could report to training camp two weeks late.

New York's defensemen stop 49er Hugh McElhenny.

When the Rams refused, Robustelli threatened to sit out the season at home. In short order, the Rams traded him to the Giants, a move that was to have happy consequences for New York.

In his third year Howell at last had assembled a team that was ready to bid for the NFL title. In the locker room before the season opener against San Francisco, Howell told the players that he thought they were finally a championship team. The Giants responded by winning, 38-21. Young Don Heinrich threw two touchdown passes, and Webster, Triplett and Gifford all picked up a great deal of yardage with outstanding running.

The Giants' pleasure was short-lived, though. The following week New York lost to the Chicago Cardinals, 35-27. During the game Cardinal coach Ray Richards had the advantage of direct communication with his quarterback. He had set up an elaborate transistor radio system which enabled him to transmit plays from the bench.

The Giants' next game was played against the Cleveland Browns, who also used electronic transmitting gear. In past seasons Cleveland coach Paul Brown had substituted a guard on virtually every play to relay instructions to the quarterback. But for the 1956 season Brown decided to equip his quarterback with a helmet containing a radio receiving set. And from the sideline Brown could broadcast an unceasing flow of advice by short-wave frequency.

New York, instead of putting a receiving unit in the quarterback's head gear, gave one to Bob Topp, a reserve end, and Filipski, a former member of the Browns. These two tuned in on Coach Brown's wave length and, on Cleveland's first play of the game, they heard him advise quarterback George Ratterman to try a pitchout to the left. They relayed the information to defensive coach Landry, who in turn shouted a warning to the Giants on the field. As a result, New York threw the Cleveland runner for a two-yard loss. So it went until Brown became aware of the eavesdropping. Then he put his microphone aside, but it was too late.

On offense the Giant ball carriers picked up 256 yards. Webster proved that he was an NFL-caliber runner by gaining 94 yards in 16 carries. Triplett picked up 91 yards, and converted back Gifford gained 73.

The defense was superb, too. Cleveland had decided to work on rookie Huff, but Sam repeatedly threw the Browns' fullback, Ed "Big Mo" Modzelewski (brother of New York's Dick Modzelewski), for a loss. Defensive end Robustelli ruined the Browns' passing game by breaking through six times to dump Ratterman for a total loss of 60 yards. The Giants won, 21-6.

After the game, Brown claimed he used the radio on only the first two plays because the sound of the crowd drowned out the signal. The Giants raised their eyebrows and laughed. They knew that the Cleveland coach did not like to admit that he had been outwitted. Two days later, NFL Commissioner Bert Bell barred the use of electronic coaching devices. "It's a good thing," said electronic defenseman Topp. "If the trend continued, the number-one draft choice of the Giants next year would have been the valedictorian of M.I.T."

In their first home game of the season, New York faced Pittsburgh. A crowd of 48,108 people

New York's Gene Filipski (40) and Jim Katcavage (82) stop Lowell Perry of the Steelers, causing him to lose his helmet, but not the ball.

filled Yankee Stadium (where the team played its home games after the Polo Grounds had been torn down). It was the largest opening-day crowd in Giant history. In the past Conerly had usually played his best when on the road, but against the Steelers that day he put on an outstanding performance. With the Giants trailing, 3-0, Conerly threw a 14-yard touchdown pass to MacAfee. Shortly after he threw a 21-yard pass to Webster for another touchdown. At the half, the Giants led, 17-3. Conerly didn't stop after intermission, either. His passing set up additional scoring drives, one of them a 27-yard touchdown pass to Rote. The final score was 38-10.

Conerly was in excellent form against Philadelphia, too. After New York's Ben Agajanian had kicked two field goals to give the Giants a 6-3 lead, Charlie went to work. At the New York 37, he gave the ball to Gifford for four yards. On the next play, Gifford carried the ball again, this time breaking free for 37 yards. Webster gained another two; then Conerly passed to MacAfee for 14 yards, which put the ball on the two. Webster drove through for the touchdown and, with the extra

Frank Gifford (16) tries to outreach Eagle Tom Scott for Mel Triplett's fumble.

point, the score was 13-3. Conerly got the "insur-ance" touchdown by throwing a 20-yard pass to Gifford. New York won, 20-13.

Afterward, Gifford and Conerly laughed about an unusual play that had developed during the game. Conerly had faked a hand-off to Webster, given the ball to Gifford and stepped back to watch the play. When the hole Gifford was heading for closed, Gifford spun around, saw Conerly and flipped the ball to him. The 32-year-old Conerly was no runner and was tackled immediately. Back in the huddle, he said to Gifford, "What was that for, Frank? I didn't want the ball."

"Charlie," said Gifford, laughing, "I was just trying to protect my rushing average."

Playing Pittsburgh again, New York won its fourth game in a row. In the first quarter, line-backer Svoboda recovered a fumble on Pitts-burgh's 25 to set the Giants up for a scoring drive. They quickly moved the ball to the one, from which Webster fought his way into the end zone. Agajanian's field goal shortly afterwards brought the score to 10-0. Pittsburgh succeeded in narrow-ing the gap to 10-7 and was threatening to score again, but Svoboda came through with another cru-cial play. He intercepted quarterback Ted Marchi-broda's pass in the end zone, thus shutting off a Steeler drive. Then the Giants marched 80 yards upfield in 15 plays, and Conerly passed to Rote for the touchdown. New York hung on to win by a score of 17-14.

Next on the schedule were the Cardinals, the only team that had beaten the Giants so far this season. Both teams had a record of five wins and one loss and were tied for the lead in the Eastern Conference. Neither could afford to lose. That afternoon, a record crowd of 62,410 gathered, and it wasn't long before they had something to shout about. As Chicago's Dave Mann was attempting to punt from his end zone, Robustelli burst through to block the kick. Mann recovered the ball, but the Giants dropped him in the end zone for a two-point safety. In the second period New York added seven points to the score when Heinrich hit Mac-Afee on a roll-out pass for two yards and a touchdown. At halftime, the score was 9-3.

Then Conerly showed the New York crowd what he could do. In the third quarter, he passed to Gifford for 48 yards to the New York 12. Next he threw a scoring pass to Webster. Later, he and Gifford teamed up for a 42-yard pass play that put the ball on the Chicago 25. Three plays later, he threw to Gifford again for 11 yards and the touchdown.

On defense, linebacker Huff keyed on Ollie Matson, the number two rusher in the NFL, and held him to 43 yards in 13 carries. The final score was 23-10.

In the showdown game, New York had been too much for the Cardinals. The Giants were alone in first place. They were flying high—or so it seemed.

The following Sunday the Washington Redskins brought them down to earth. The Giants did nothing right that afternoon as the Redskins ran wild. The final score was 33-7. New York maintained its hold on first place only because the Chicago Cardinals also lost. But Howell let his team know that they wouldn't be in first place much longer if they didn't play more fiercely.

The Giants hit hard when they played the Chicago Bears the next week. With time running out they led, 17-10. The defense had done a remarkable job in containing the Chicago rushing game (the Bears gained only 12 yards that day). On their part, the Giants' runners had ripped through Chicago's line for 176 yards. It seemed like another New York victory, but Howell's team hadn't anticipated the performance of Harlon Hill, the Chicago end from Florence Teachers College. With one minute and 50 seconds remaining in the game, Bear quarterback Ed Brown threw deep to Hill. The pass appeared overthrown, but Hill tipped the ball with the ends of his fingers. Sliding onto his belly, he made a diving catch in the end zone to tie the game, 17-17. It was an unfortunate ending for the Giants, but they were still leading

Alex Webster narrowly misses a pass from Giant quarterback Don Heinrich during the Bears' game, which ended in a 17-17 tie.

the Eastern Conference.

The Redskins were waiting to knock them out of first place, but this time the Giants solved the problem of the Washington defense. While standing on the sideline with Assistant Coach Lombardi, Conerly decided that Washington linebacker La-Vern Torgeson could be exploited. Torgeson, anxious to make every tackle, was overcommitting himself. So when Torgeson abandoned his territory to blitz, Conerly passed over him or used "trap" plays. (In a trap play a guard will brush block a defensive lineman; that is, he will hit him lightly and let him slip by. Then the guard from the other end of the line will pull out and cross over to hit the opposing lineman from the side, creating a hole through which the runner can carry the ball.) When Torgeson stayed at his spot, the Giants double-blocked and ran over him.

Gifford continued to justify the coaches' decision to switch him to the offense. In the first quarter, he took a pitchout from Heinrich, headed wide to the right, suddenly stopped and threw the ball to MacAfee for 29 yards and a touchdown. After that, Gifford ran for three more touchdowns, and New York avenged its earlier 33-7 loss to Washington with a 28-7 victory.

The Giants were closing in on the conference title, but Howell warned them they could not let up. The Cardinals and the Redskins were within striking distance. And when the Giants lost to Cleveland, 24-7, the race became even closer. But New York had worked too hard for the championship to lose it now.

In the last game, the Giants played Philadelphia. Gifford threw to Rote for the first touchdown, then ran 10 yards for the next score. Webster rushed seven yards for the final touchdown. In all, Giant rushers gained 291 yards that afternoon, and the final score was 21-7. More important, New York won the Eastern Conference championship and a chance to play Chicago for the NFL title.

For Howell, the conference title was indeed satisfying. When he had taken over as New York's coach, there had been many who doubted that he was the right man. They had pointed out his mediocre records while coaching at Wagner College. But Howell had answered his critics by making the right decisions at New York. His faith in Conerly had been justified. During the 1956 campaign, Conerly had completed 90 of 174 passes for 1,143 yards and 10 touchdowns. In addition, Gifford's performance had proved the wisdom of converting him to an offensive halfback. Gifford had rushed for 819 yards and five touchdowns, caught 51 passes for five touchdowns and completed two of five passes—both for touchdowns. Webster had shown he could run the football in any league by carrying 178 times for 694 yards and seven touchdowns.

Although the conference championship was satisfying, Howell and the Giants knew that it would be nothing compared with the thrill of winning the NFL title. So they began their preparations for the all-important game.

There was more to getting ready than just working out. Three days before the game, Andy Robustelli heard the weather report, which predicted freezing temperatures, and decided that he'd better telephone Frank Yohan, a district manager for a company that manufactured basketball shoes.

"Frank," he said, "I've been thinking. If the weather stays this cold, we'll be playing Sunday's game on ice as hard as cement. All the players have basketball shoes, but they're old ones and the rubber soles must be pretty well dried out. Would fresh gum soles on brand new shoes grab the ground better?"

"You bet they would," said Yohan.

So Robustelli, who owned a sporting goods store, asked him to deliver four dozen pairs of the special shoes, which he put aside for his Giant teammates. On the day of the game, Robustelli's foresight paid off. An hour-and-a-half before the opening kickoff, Howell sent Ed Hughes and Gene Filipski out to test the field. Hughes wore cleated shoes and Filipski wore rubber-soled sneakers that Robustelli had provided. Hughes took a few steps and slipped. As a result, rubber-soled sneakers were issued to the Giants.

Treacherous footing was only one problem the players faced. The weather also made it difficult for them to hold onto the football. The temperature was so cold (20 degrees) that the mimeographing machine in the press box at Yankee Stadium froze. The fans in the bleacher seats found one way to deal with the cold—they gathered around a small trash fire until the police made them put out the flames. The players couldn't resort to trash fires, but all of them made sure to put on long underwear to combat the freezing temperatures. Conerly wore full-length golf gloves on the advice of a fellow Mississippian who was playing for the Edmonton Eskimoes in Canada. During the game, however, he discarded them after fumbling.

For a team that had not won a championship since 1938, the Giants were not particularly tense in the locker room. About 1 P.M. the players were laughing and joking and generally displaying what Coach Howell afterwards called, "too much levity." He said, "I always thought players should be quiet before the big game. At least that's the way we always were when I played."

The Giants may have had an unusual way of getting ready for a big ball game, but no one could argue with the results. New York wasted no time in putting the numbers on the scoreboard. Filipski took George Blanda's kickoff on the eight and ran 53 yards to the Chicago 39. Three plays later, Heinrich connected on a 21-yard pass to Gifford at the 17. From there, on an off-tackle play, Triplett drove a couple of Bears and an official who'd gotten in the way right into the end zone. After the addition of the extra point, the score was Giants 7, Bears 0.

Slightly more than two minutes later, Bear fullback Rick Casares fumbled and Robustelli recovered the ball on the Chicago 15. With Conerly leading the attack now, the Giants attempted another drive into the end zone. This time the Bears' line stiffened and New York settled for a 17-yard field goal by Ben Agajanian. The score was 10-0.

It wasn't long before the Giants' defense came up with another crucial play. Defensive back Patton intercepted a pass from the Bears' Ed Brown and returned the ball 26 yards to the Chicago 37. When the Giants' drive stalled, Agajanian booted a 43-yard field goal, his longest of the year.

The Giants continued to pick up scoring momentum during the half. Webster concluded a

During the championship game, fullback Mel Triplett drives into the end zone, bowling over an official in the process.

Giant drive early in the second period by going over from the three-yard line for the touchdown. A few minutes later, the former NFL reject drove over the goal line from the one. And when the Giants blocked a punt shortly before the first half ended, rookie defensive back Henry Moore recovered the ball in the end zone to give New York another touchdown and a 34-7 lead.

In the last half Conerly continued to do a masterful job of directing the Giants' attack. He threw a nine-yard touchdown pass to Rote, then a 14-yard pass to Gifford for another score. In all, Conerly completed seven of 10 passes for 195 yards. The final score was New York 47, Chicago 7.

The Giants had put on a devastating performance. As the players trotted off the field, the crowd of 56,836 persons roared their approval. The fans' response must have been especially gratifying for Conerly, who, not many seasons before, had been the special target of their abuse.

It had taken three years to build a championship team, but Giant fans considered the time well spent. Many of the nearly frozen New York partisans came pouring onto the field. They shattered the goal posts in the kind of enthusiastic display the city hadn't seen since the Bears and Giants played at the old Polo Grounds in 1934. The frenzied Giant fans even ripped Huff's jersey from his back. But Sam didn't mind. He was too busy savor-

Alex Webster drives over the goal line during the

second period of the title game.

ing victory—as were his teammates. Weary and dirty, they shouted the nonsensical exaggerations that are a victor's privilege. And they kept right on shouting at the victory party that evening, where Conerly kept repeating, "Do you realize we're champions of the world? That covers a mighty lot of territory."

BALTIMORE
COLTS
1958

In 1946 a new league, called the All-America Football Conference, began to compete with the NFL. Because the new league failed to gain sufficient public interest, it lasted only three years. When the NFL merged with the All-America Conference in 1949, the Baltimore Colts and two other AAC teams were grudgingly admitted to the league. By 1951, however, the Colts were bankrupt and the franchise had to be surrendered. For two years the city was without football, but the people of Baltimore persisted in their desire for a franchise. During the two-year NFL blackout, the Colt Marching Band—127 members strong—practiced every week, making it the only football band in America without a team. And for two years Baltimore worked hard to get back its team.

In 1953, Carroll Rosenbloom, an energetic businessman, raised the capital to purchase the defunct Dallas Texans and brought them to Baltimore. From University Place down to East Baltimore Street, the city celebrated the return of the Colts. Photos of Baltimore players appeared in the windows of taverns, groceries and department stores. Billboards were plastered with pro-Colt sentiments. A doll-sized model of a Colt player, complete with a bobbling head, became a standard item in the rear window of every Colt fan's car. The new team tentatively offered 15,000 season tickets, and before the new year was well under way, it had sold all of them.

Unfortunately, the team at first was not quite as ready as its fans. In 1953 the Colts won only three games and lost nine. It was not a good start, but Colt fans didn't mind. Now that they had their football team back, they felt that the Colts would soon be winners. But 1954 was not to be the Colts' year either. Under their new coach, Weeb Ewbank, the team again won only three and lost nine, but there were encouraging signs. The Colts had won two of their last three games, and they had done well in the annual draft of college players. The newcomers included fullback Alan Ameche, end Raymond Berry, halfback L. G. Dupre, quarterback George Shaw, linebacker Jack Patera, center linebacker Dick Szymanski and offensive tackle George Preas. The new men helped, and in 1955 the Colts showed a big improvement by winning five, losing six and tying one.

That same year John Constantine Unitas was playing for the Bloomfield Rams, a semipro team located just outside of Pittsburgh. He received only $6.00 a game, which was far less than he had expected to earn when he tried out with the Pittsburgh Steelers before the beginning of the season. But the Steelers had released him, so Unitas took the opportunity to play with the Bloomfield Rams in order to keep his quarterbacking skills sharp. He hadn't given up his dreams of being an NFL star.

Unitas was used to being rejected. Although he had starred as a quarterback at St. Justin's High School in Pittsburgh, he had been turned down for scholarships by Notre Dame and Indiana. And they were the only two major colleges that had given him a tryout. "I only weighed 145 pounds then," Unitas later recalled, "and I guess that didn't impress 'em too much."

Eventually, he was offered a scholarship by the University of Louisville, where he passed for 3,000 yards and 27 touchdowns during his varsity career. Still, the pros were not particularly impressed by Unitas. He was drafted on the ninth round by the Steelers, who gave him a brief tryout in training camp before releasing him. Later, while playing with Bloomfield, Unitas made plans for getting into the NFL. Then one day in February, 1956, Baltimore general manager Don Kellett called him long distance and said that the Colts would like him to come to their rookie camp in Westminster, Maryland.

When Unitas arrived at the Colts' training camp, the team was much stronger than it had been in preceding years, especially on defense. To assist veterans Gino Marchetti, Don Joyce, and Art Donovan, Ewbank had acquired from the Rams Gene Lipscomb, a 6-foot 6-inch, 288-pound tackle who was called "Big Daddy." Big Daddy Lipscomb was a colorful addition to the Colts' defensive line. Ewbank would later describe his tackling technique in the following way: "He sorts the backs out and when he comes to the ball carrier, that's the one he keeps."

Although the defense was sound, the offense lacked scoring punch. This weakness gave Unitas his chance, and he made good. He survived both the rookie camp and the regular training camp. When the season started he was on the Colts' roster, even though he was sitting on the bench. He was not disheartened about being a substitute because he realized that few players can move from a team like the Bloomfield Rams to the Baltimore Colts in one short season.

Naturally, Unitas was waiting for an opportunity to show his skills in a game. His hopes were realized when, shortly after the 1956 season started, regular quarterback George Shaw suffered a leg injury in a game against the Chicago Bears. Unitas was suddenly tossed into the front lines.

Unfortunately, his first pass was intercepted. In the last half, he mishandled the ball so badly that the Colts' fumbles cost them the game.

Unitas improved after that, however. He threw two touchdown passes against Green Bay in a 28-21 Baltimore victory, and passed for three touchdowns in a 56-21 romp over Los Angeles. But late in the season the Colts lost three in a row, and the rumor began to circulate that Ewbank would be fired after the team's last game, which would be played against the Washington Redskins. Owner Rosenbloom refused to confirm the rumor, simply saying that he would wait until the season was over before making any decision concerning Ewbank. Fortunately, Baltimore won the game on a long pass from Unitas to Jim Mutscheller, and Ewbank still had a job.

Although the Colts had the same coach the next season, to many players Ewbank didn't seem like the same man. He started the season by imposing a tighter discipline on the team. In order to get his players in superior condition he worked them harder in training camp than he had in the past. He demanded that they concentrate on football, and to make sure they did, he instituted early curfews and fined players who violated them.

Ewbank was being stricter with the Colts because he realized that if Unitas lived up to his promise, Baltimore could become a championship team. And by driving the team harder, the coach was trying to make sure the opportunity didn't slip away.

During his first full season as a pro, Unitas built up an impressive record. In 12 games, he completed 172 of 301 passes for 2,550 yards and 24 touchdowns. He threw at least one touchdown pass in every game. When he didn't throw the ball, he directed the rushing game with all the poise of a veteran. In 1957, the former NFL discard nearly led the Colts to a Western Conference title. Going into its last two games, Baltimore was tied with the San Francisco 49ers and the Detroit Lions. But Unitas could not take the team all the way. The Colts lost their last two games to finish the season with a record of seven wins and five losses, behind both champion Detroit and runner-up San Francisco.

But now the team was convinced of its ability to win the championship. As the 1958 season started, the city swelled with excitement. Season tickets were treasures in Baltimore. Individual game tickets were also difficult to obtain. On Sundays when games were played at home, a local radio station would make announcements about tickets that had suddenly become available. Colt fans who were listening would telephone the owners and then rush about town to secure the tickets.

Ewbank had assembled a real powerhouse. In an off-season trade, he had gotten Ray Krouse, a defensive tackle, who could relieve Lipscomb and Donovan when necessary. To his linebacking corps of Don Shinnick, Bill Pellington, Patera and Doug Eggers, he added Leo Sanford, obtained in a trade with the Chicago Cardinals. Rookies Johnny Sample and Ray Brown—playing with Milt Davis, Andy Nelson, Carl Taseff and Bert Reichichar—added depth to the Baltimore defensive secondary.

The offense now was just as strong. Unitas' bodyguards on the blocking line included Art Spinney, Buzz Nutter, Alex Sandusky, Preas and Jim Parker. Parker, whose thighs measured 29 inches around, was especially skillful at keeping rushing defensive ends away from Unitas. For receivers, Unitas had flanker Lenny Moore and ends Mutscheller and Berry. Besides catching a ball, Moore could also run with it. In 1957, his second year in the NFL, he had gained 488 yards rushing. Mutscheller also was more than just a pass receiver—he was an especially good blocker. Berry was not as diversified in his football talents as either Moore or Mutscheller, but nobody on the

Quarterback Unitas with his favorite receiver, Ray Berry.

team could match his pass-catching ability.

In 1954 the Colts had taken Berry in the 20th round of the college draft, expecting very little from him. But Berry fooled them. In 1957, he and Unitas had proved to be a deadly combination: Berry caught 47 passes for 800 yards and six touchdowns. And he did it despite certain physical handicaps. Berry had eye trouble, but to compensate for it he wore extra-large contact lenses. He was not a very strong man either, but he worked at his position until he perfected all his moves. To strengthen his hands, he manipulated a ball of resilient "silly putty" an hour a day. He would do anything to improve. For catching a football was his passion. Berry once said: "When I was just out of high school in an eastern Texas town called Paris, I went to see a movie called *Crazylegs* five times. It was about Elroy Hirsch, who played end at the time for the Los Angeles Rams, and I decided that the thing I wanted to do most in the world was to catch passes for a professional football team the way Hirsch did."

Passing wasn't the Colts' only strong point. For offensive balance, Unitas could give the ball to several fine runners. Besides Moore, there were halfbacks L. G. Dupre and Lenny Lyles (a sprint-fast rookie) and fullback Ameche. In three years with the Colts, Ameche had gained 2,313 yards with a crushing style that earned him the name "The Horse." Dupre's style was more elusive and, though the initials L. G. stood for Louis George, Baltimore fans called him "Long Gone" for his breakaway runs.

The Colts could boast a strong defense, plus skilled runners and receivers, but they depended mainly on Unitas. On opening day, before 48,377 ecstatic Baltimore fans, Unitas showed just how important he was. He passed the ball 43 times for 23 completions. Berry caught 10 of his passes for 149 yards and two touchdowns. Unitas was at his best in the clutch. With the Colts trailing, 15-

14, in the final quarter, he led them to two more touchdowns, and Baltimore won, 28-15.

The following week, it was Lenny Moore's turn to give an outstanding performance. He scored four times in Baltimore's 51-38 victory over the Chicago Bears. Moore got two touchdowns on runs of 28 and nine yards, and he scored the other pair on passes of 77 and 33 yards from Unitas. Baltimore's defense intercepted five passes, two each by Ray Brown and Bill Pellington. In the wild offensive battle both teams scored on long kickoff returns: 103 yards by the Colts' Lyles, 99 yards by the Bears' Willie Gallimore.

Green Bay was next on the schedule, and the Packers were well prepared for the game. They jumped out to a 17-0 lead, but Baltimore refused to be cowed by the Packer attack. Calmly, Unitas set about to catch up. In the second half he launched a comeback by hitting Mutscheller with a touchdown pass of 54 yards. That was just the beginning. In all, he completed 16 of 35 passes for 238 yards. The Colts rallied to win, 24-17.

Baltimore continued to win by beating Detroit, 40-14, in an explosive offensive display. The Colts accumulated 535 yards from scrimmage. Moore bolted for 136 yards in 12 carries, one of them an 11-yard touchdown run. Unitas completed 11 of 17 passes for 221 yards, including a 37-yard touchdown pass to Mutscheller. Meanwhile, Baltimore's defense, with Big Daddy and company at their best, limited the Lions to 79 yards on the ground.

The Redskins were the Colts' next victim. Although Unitas did not have one of his best days, he still managed to complete a 48-yard touchdown pass to Berry. Rookie halfback Lyles gave Unitas valuable assistance by running 101 yards with a kickoff to put the game out of reach for Washington, 28-10. The final score was 35-10.

Alan Ameche contributes a touchdown to the Colts' 40-14 victory over Detroit.

The Colts had been fired up for the game by, of all people, Redskin owner George Preston Marshall, who had a history of saying the wrong thing at the wrong time. Marshall, who was also noted for his temper, had not been able to control it when the Colts kidded him in blunt locker-room fashion at a midweek banquet in Baltimore. The players resented the way Marshall tried to "pull rank" on them, and they resolved to pay him back —on the field.

In a return game with the Packers, Baltimore left no doubts that it was the better team. The game was played in a steady, driving rain, but nothing could stop the Colts that day—not even the loss of their quarterback. Unitas left the contest after being hurt badly on a quarterback sneak at the end of the first half. He had been lying face down on the ground after being tackled, when an over-enthusiastic player slammed down on him from behind, and his knees smashed into Johnny's unprotected lower back. Unitas suffered fractured ribs and a punctured lung on the play, and was finished for the afternoon. Many feared he was finished for the season.

George Shaw took over for Unitas, and did a superb job. He completed 10 of 13 passes, three for touchdowns. Five interceptions helped the Colts roll up the score, 56-0, for the first shutout ever recorded by Baltimore.

Shaw also did a creditable job against the New York Giants the next week, but, without Unitas, the Colts ended their winning streak at six games. Shaw threw three touchdown passes, but toward the end of the game the Colts trailed by three points. When Shaw attempted to pass for the winning touchdown, Giant linebacker Sam Huff intercepted. The final score was 24-21.

The loss reduced the Colts' lead over the second-place Chicago Bears to one game, a margin the Bears might eliminate in the head-to-head confrontation of the two teams the next week. But the inspired Baltimore defense held Chicago to a total of 161 yards in rushing and passing. And for the first time in 149 games the Bears did not score. Shaw was in charge of the Colts' attack once again, and he completed 10 of 23 passes for 131 yards and a touchdown to Berry. The most important player in the Colts' offense, however, was Alan Ameche, who rushed for 142 yards in 26 carries. The final score was 17-0, Baltimore's second shutout in two weeks.

With only four games to go, the Colts and their breathless admirers prepared to enter the home stretch. The outlook for the team improved with the report that Unitas could return to action. Although he was not entirely healed, he wanted to get back into the line-up. He felt that he hadn't worked his way up from the Bloomfield Rams just

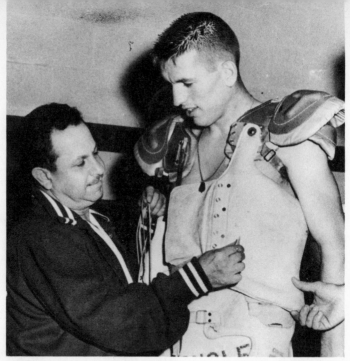

Trainer Ed Block helps Unitas into a special steel-and-foam-rubber harness prior to the Colts' game with the Rams.

to watch his team from the sidelines.

Before the Colts' game with the Los Angeles Rams, trainer Ed Block and his assistant, Dimiter Spasoff, helped Unitas into a special steel-and-foam-rubber harness designed to protect him. Unitas didn't waste any time proving his fitness to the Rams. On the Colts' first play from scrimmage, he threw a 58-yard touchdown pass to Lenny Moore. He also hit Mutscheller for a 12-yard touchdown.

Even though Unitas was hitting his receivers, the Colts led by a slim margin, 13-7, as they went

into the last period. But they capitalized on interceptions and fumbles to win, 34-7. Unitas had
completed 12 of 18 passes for a total of 218 yards.
Lenny Moore had caught seven of them for 162
yards.

The game had been extremely difficult for Unitas. Los Angeles had hit him hard to find out if
he could take the pain. The Rams felt that if they
could get him out of the game early, their chances
of winning would be improved considerably. But
Unitas did not shy away from contact. Twice, in
fact, he completed passes with eager Ram tacklers
actually draped over his body. When he left the
field late in the game with a cut over his right eye
and blood coming from a torn lip, the crowd of
57,557 in Baltimore's Memorial Stadium stood and
roared their approval.

With only three games remaining in the season,
the Colts led the rest of the Western Conference.
But they weren't cocky. They remembered that
in the previous season they had lost their last two
games and a chance to win the conference title.
Thus, they were well prepared for the contest
against the San Francisco 49ers. But for the first
30 minutes of the game they played badly. The
49ers left the field at half time leading, 27-7.

It seemed that the Colts would fade at season's
end once again. They didn't, however, and Unitas
was the reason. He rallied his team for 21 decisive

Ray Berry is about to catch a pass from Unitas in spite of the efforts of a Los Angeles defender to break it up.

points in the last quarter, running for one score and passing for another. In all, he completed 17 of 33 passes for 229 yards. Berry's receiving (nine passes for 114 yards) and Moore's running (eight carries for 114 yards) also helped. A brilliant 73-yard touchdown run by Moore put the Colts in front to stay. The final score was 28-27.

The victory gave the Colts the Western Conference championship, and now Baltimore fans waited to see who would win in the East. Although the Colts lost their two remaining games with the Rams and the 49ers, the losses had no effect on the championship. The NFL title game was all that mattered to the team. And it was all that mattered to the citizens of Baltimore, who became highly excited over the coming game.

The Giants won the Eastern Conference championship, and the NFL title game was scheduled for Yankee Stadium. After several days of bitter cold, the crucial Sunday brought crisp autumn weather to New York City for what would later be called the greatest NFL championship game ever. There were indications even before the game that it was going to be a strange day. With 40 million people prepared to watch the game on television, a fan in the park accidentally kicked loose the power plug leading to the television cameras. His misstep darkened the sets of 40 million viewers—for just a short time, however.

Meanwhile, in the Baltimore dressing room, Ewbank was getting his team fired up. In his pre-game talk, the coach pointed out that 14 of the players gathered before him had been rejected by other clubs before joining the Colts. The speech was calm in tone, but its impact was tremendous.

At the start of the game, it seemed as though the Colts would score first. Unitas sent Moore out on a sideline pass pattern. The Giants had only one man covering him, and that was a mistake. Unitas hit Moore with a pass at the New York 40, and Lenny carried the ball to the 25 before he was brought down. Here the tough Giant defense dug in and held the Colts. Ewbank decided to try a field goal by Steve Myhra. But linebacker Huff blocked the kick, and the majority of the 64,185 fans in Yankee Stadium cheered.

Now it was New York's turn. Quarterback Charlie Conerly hit fullback Mel Triplett with a pass at the New York 31. Then halfback Frank Gifford ran for 38 yards to the Baltimore 31. The Giants were driving hard, but the Baltimore defense met the challenge and forced New York to attempt a field goal. Pat Summerall's kick from the 36-yard line was good. New York led, 3-0.

In the second quarter, Big Daddy Lipscomb helped the Colts get on the scoreboard. He recovered a fumble by Gifford on the New York 20. Unitas decided to attempt the touchdown on the ground. Ameche and Moore took turns carrying the ball, and Ameche drove in for the touchdown from the two-yard line. The score: Baltimore 7, New York 3.

The Colts were gathering momentum now. They started their next drive on their own 14. Unitas, for the most part, kept the ball on the ground, and he passed only twice—both times to Berry. The second completion was good for 15 yards and a touchdown. At the half time Baltimore led, 14-3.

It was a hard-fought game, and emotions on both sides were high. In fact, just before the half

Players on both teams scramble to recover a fumble by New York's Frank Gifford. Ray Krouse (at right) finally recovered the ball for the Colts.

An official tries to break up the clash between Sam Huff (70) and Coach Ewbank (at left).

ended, Ewbank had become angry at the way Huff had tackled Berry out of bounds on a pass play. After harsh words were exchanged, Ewbank suddenly hit Huff on the jaw. Huff tried to get at the Baltimore coach, but Colt players restrained him.

Ewbank was still fired up at half time in the locker room. He wasn't satisfied with a 14-3 lead. "You've got to assume we're two touchdowns behind instead of 11 points ahead," he said. "That's the only way to play it. Go out there and get two more touchdowns because you need them. Don't go out thinking that all you have to do is protect your lead."

Ewbank had anticipated that the Giants' offense would begin to click, and he was right. The Giants scored their first touchdown as the result of a lucky break. Conerly threw a long pass to Kyle Rote, who had gone down the sideline and had then cut to the middle, where he caught the ball on the Colts' 45. He ran with it to the 25 before defensive back Andy Nelson jarred the ball loose. Here, Giant halfback Alex Webster, trailing the play, scooped up the ball and headed for the goal line. The other Colt defensive halfback, Carl Taseff, caught Webster half a stride from the goal line and kept him from scoring. The Giants had moved from their own 13 to the Baltimore one. On the next play Triplett drove through for the score. The Colts' lead had been cut to four points.

Now the crowd was roaring, "Go Giants! Go Giants! Go Giants!" In the final quarter, Conerly switched from Rote and Gifford as his favorite targets to Bob Schnelker. First he hit Schnelker with a 17-yard pass. Then he connected with another for 46 yards, which put the ball on the Baltimore 15. With the Colts' defense concentrating on Schnelker, Conerly threw to Gifford on the five. Gifford carried the ball in for the score, and New York went ahead, 17-14.

The course of the game had reversed itself. Earlier, the Giants had appeared beaten. But a lucky break gave them a lift, and now New York was picking up momentum. When Unitas got the ball, the Giants swamped him. First, defensive end Andy Robustelli stormed in and threw him for an 11-yard loss. Then defensive tackle Dick Modzelewski threw him for a nine-yard loss. The Colts had to punt.

The Giants returned the Colt kick to the 19, and then gave the ball to their runners. On the first down Webster was stopped after gaining only one yard. But Gifford made five the next play. It was a crucial third-down situation. If Conerly could only make a first down, the Giants could win by letting the clock run out. Baltimore's only chance was to stop the Giants and force them to kick. Conerly gave the ball to Gifford again, but the Colts' Marchetti tackled him just short of a first down. In fact Marchetti hit Gifford so violently that he broke his own ankle, and had to be carried from the field. The Giants did not gamble; they kicked the ball to the Colts.

When the Colts got the ball on their own 14, less than two minutes remained to play in the game. But Unitas was used to working under pressure. He had pulled games out of the fire before, and he thought he could do it again. The Giants' strategy was to prevent Unitas from hitting Moore with a long pass. This failed to stop Unitas, however. He knew that the Giants' defense would be playing back to guard against his long throws. As a result, he could use his short-pass patterns to move his team into scoring position.

The Giants hurried Unitas, causing his first pass to fall incomplete. His next one was aimed at Dupre, who dropped the ball. It was now third down and 10—an obvious passing situation—and the Giants prepared to defend against another aerial attack. But Unitas crossed them. He gave the ball to Moore, who ran for the first down with a yard to spare.

Then Unitas went back to passing. Three times he failed to hit his receivers. Then he began to find them. He connected on three passes in a row to put the ball at midfield. There were 64 seconds left when Baltimore took time out to stop the clock.

With the pressure on, Unitas hit Berry at the 35, then again at the 13. Into the game ran field-goal kicker Myhra. Only seven seconds were left to play when he kicked a 20-yard field goal to tie the score, 17-17, and send the game into overtime. It was the first overtime situation in the history of NFL title games.

Officials held a coin toss at the end of the regulation game, and the Giants won and elected to receive. Since the first team to score would win, New York wanted possession of the ball. All they needed was a field goal.

Don Maynard took the kickoff and returned it to the New York 20. A run by Gifford and a pass by Conerly both failed. On third down, as the Giants' quarterback faded back to pass, he saw that he had running room, so he began to run. For a moment, it seemed as if he'd gain the first down. But the Colts stopped him a foot short, and New York's Don Chandler had to kick.

Baltimore took the ball on the 20. There was no clock to worry about now. Unitas merely had to get the Colts on the scoreboard again—any way he could. His first play was an end run, and Dupre carried the ball to the 30 for the first down. On the next play, Unitas gambled on hitting Moore deep along the sideline, but New York's Lindon Crow tipped the ball away. After that, Dupre picked up three yards. Then Unitas hit Ameche with a pass that gave the Colts a first down on their own 40.

Unitas went back to the play he had called when the Colts took possession of the ball, and sent Dupre on a sweep to the right. Dupre gained yardage, but not enough for the first down. On the next play, Modzelewski dropped Unitas for an eight-yard loss.

Unitas' next play was one of the keys in the

drive. He brought the Colts out in a formation that had not been used that afternoon. Moore was a slot back to the right (that is, he was positioned behind the gap between the end and the tackle on the right side of the line) and both ends were "split" (which means they were positioned at least six yards outside the tackles). When Unitas faded back, he was looking for Moore. But the Giants had Moore covered, so he looked for Berry. Fortunately, the Giant back covering Berry had slipped, and now Unitas waved his receiver to proceed downfield. Coolly, he completed the pass for the first down at the New York 42.

COLTS' FORMATION

Two factors prompted Unitas to call the next play. First, Modzelewski was coming across the line aggressively, and he could be trapped. Second, Huff, who had been keying his moves on Ameche, had dropped back from the line, obviously expecting a pass. So Unitas gave the ball to Ameche on a draw play (in which the quarterback

With his head lowered, fullback Alan Ameche charges through a hole in the Giants' line for the winning touchdown.

drops back as if to pass, but instead hands the ball to one of his backs, who moves straight ahead past onrushing defenders), and The Horse sped through for 23 yards to the Giant 21-yard line.

The Colts were near enough for Myhra to boot a field goal, but Unitas wanted to get even closer. He gave the ball to Dupre once again on the sweep, but this time the Giants stopped the play for no gain. A quick pass to Berry, who was running diagonally over the middle, resulted in a first down at the nine. Now Ameche made a yard, staying in the middle of the field so that a field goal could be kicked easily. At this point Unitas made a daring call.

The Giants were bunched together to stop another smash at the line, but Unitas fooled them. He sent Mutscheller slanting wide to the sideline and lofted the ball over the head of linebacker Cliff Livingston. Mutscheller caught it at the one. On the next play, Ameche carried the ball in for the touchdown. Baltimore had won the sudden-death overtime, 23-17, in the most dramatic finish in the history of NFL championship games. And now the Colts celebrated.

The locker room was a madhouse as reporters crowded around Unitas, Berry, Ameche, and the others. "It's the greatest thing that ever happened,"

Jubilant Baltimore fans swarm over the bus carrying the victorious Colts.

Berry was shouting. "Who outgutted who?" Big Daddy wanted to know. The other Colts were happy to oblige with the answer. Seated in front of his dressing cubicle, Unitas was remembering the hard times at Bloomfield, and savoring the championship, "I just got a chance to show my stuff," he said. "That's all I've needed, but nobody gave it to me for a while." Baltimore general manager Kellett, who had called Unitas three seasons before to invite him to training camp, was saying, "The call cost us eighty cents. We've come out so far ahead, it looks like a swindle."

It certainly did, but in Baltimore the fans were toasting to that swindle. When the Colts returned home, 30,000 people greeted the team at the airport. In their enthusiasm, they smashed in the top of a police car and scrambled all over the buses which were to take the team into town. Earlier, a Colt fan, listening to the game on his car radio, had crashed into a telephone pole and was hospitalized. But for him and other Colt fans, the championship was worth almost any price.

The welcome finally reached near-riot proportions. The team decided to forget about the buses. The police started a shuttle service, running the players and their wives through the packed thousands two or three at a time in police cars, red lights flashing and sirens screaming. It was a night Baltimore would remember for a long time.

GREEN BAY
PACKERS
1961

On the first day of the Green Bay Packers' training camp in 1959, the new coach, Vince Lombardi,
called a team meeting. What he had to say startled
the Packers. As linebacker Bill Forester later remembered, "Lombardi had a football in his hand.
He looked at us and said, 'This is a football. Before
we're through with it, we're gonna run it down everybody's throat.' That took a lot of guts because
we'd won only one game the year before."

Indeed the Packer team was in bad shape when
Lombardi took over. Quarterback Bart Starr was
on the verge of quitting to join the coaching staff
at Marquette University. Packer quarterback-half-
back-fullback Paul Hornung also was thinking of
quitting. "The situation was pretty hopeless," Hornung later commented, "and I was fed up. After the

'58 season I was hoping they would trade me. I didn't know where I stood. They played me at one position one week and somewhere else the next." The morale among the rest of the team was just as bad.

So it did take courage to tell a team with a record of one win, 10 losses and one tie for the previous season that it would be cramming footballs down other people's throats shortly. But Lombardi was that kind of man. He'd proven his courage on every level of his career. When he had reported for freshman football practice at Fordham University in 1933, an assistant coach had looked him over in surprise when he said he was a tackle. Lombardi just seemed too small.

"Get in your stance," said the coach.

Vince did, and as he has recalled the scene:

"He hit the hell out of me. When he told me to get in my stance again, this time I was ready for him. I let him have it."

"Okay," said the coach. "You pass."

As a 172-pound varsity guard Lombardi was a member of the line known as the "Seven Walls of Granite." In one game he played with his mouth full of blood as a result of a collision early in the contest with a tackle named Tony Matisi. Afterwards, the team doctor had to put 30 stitches in Vince's mouth.

Lombardi demonstrated the same kind of tough-

Coach Lombardi puts the Packers through a block-ing drill.

ness in coaching. On his second day in camp, after putting the Packers through a hard practice, he found 20 players scattered about the training room waiting to be attended to for minor injuries. "What's this?" he said in his brisk, loud voice. "You've got to play with those small hurts, you know!" The next day the number of Packers in the trainer's quarters had dwindled to two. One of them, A. D. Williams, an end, had his foot in a bucket of ice in order to reduce the swelling in his ankle. "How're you feeling?" Vince boomed. Williams hopped out of his chair and said through chattering teeth, "I feel better already, coach."

Lombardi was tough on all his men—rookies and stars alike. When the great pass receiver Billy Howton told Lombardi, "If I don't get more money, I'm gonna quit," Lombardi quickly retorted, "Go ahead and quit." It required courage to release his finest pass receiver when he had no assured successor, but Lombardi did it. He wanted to establish that he was in charge. "There can be only one dominant man on a team," he said. "He has to be the coach."

He made the same point to Hornung, who called long distance to training camp two days late and said, "Coach, I didn't get my expense money."

Lombardi replied, "Haul yourself here. You get your expenses when you make my team."

During his first week at Green Bay, the coach

yelled so loudly and so often that he lost his voice. He insisted that injured players run in practice and warned, "You're preparing yourself mentally. Don't cross me. If you cross me a second time, you're gone."

Lombardi was as good as his word. Through clever trades he discarded the playboys, the shirkers and the troublemakers. Then he remodeled the spirit of those who were left. He harassed them out of the bars and into bed by curfew time. He forced them to attend meetings, meals and workouts on time. He let them know that his intentions were to make them tougher than the football players on other teams. "Football is two things," he said. "It's blocking and tackling. If you block and tackle better than the team you're playing, you win."

To get the perfect execution he wanted, Lombardi used drills aimed at getting the players to move simultaneously at the snap of the ball—hitting the blocking sled, wind sprints (20-yard dashes at full speed), one-on-one blocking and tackling practices. Lombardi's brand of football was not fancy. Where other coaches searched for their foes' weaknesses, Lombardi took the direct route. "There is no more effective way to damage a team's morale, destroy its poise," he told his players, "than to attack and gain through or over his strongest position. Beat him at his strength and his weaknesses become weaker than ever."

Lombardi drove his players hard. To make his team function properly, which is to say, perfectly, he did not allow mistakes, and he was especially intolerant of lack of effort. As Packer defensive back Hank Gremminger later would say, "Vince Lombardi works you so hard that if he told you to go to hell, you'd enjoy the trip."

Behind his back, the Packers called Lombardi *Il Duce* (the nickname for Mussolini, Italy's dictator from 1922-43) and "The Hornet." Defensive tackle Henry Jordan said of him, "The coach is very fair. He treats us all like dogs." But Lombardi paid no attention to the players' comments because he knew that his team was finally shaping up. And he was beginning to get an idea of the most suitable position for each of his men.

For one thing, he had devised a plan for Hornung. When Lombardi had first come to Green Bay, he had looked at films of past Packer games. In one film he saw a play in which Hornung ran from the halfback spot. He was impressed by the way Hornung cut at the right instant and drove with such power that the tacklers couldn't hold him.

"Run that play again," Lombardi had ordered an assistant.

Lombardi watched the play carefully a second time and liked what he saw.

"There's my offense," he said. "Paul Hornung will be my Frank Gifford." Gifford, of course, was the New York Giants' multi-threat halfback. Earlier, Lombardi had been the offensive coach for the Giants and, along with head coach Jim Lee Howell, he had converted Gifford from a defensive back to a run-pass halfback. Lombardi envisioned Hornung as the same kind of star.

Another of Lombardi's decisions made second-year man Jim Taylor the starting fullback. When Taylor joined the Packers in 1958, Ray "Scooter" McLean was the head coach. For the first 10 games of the season, Taylor did little more than return a few kickoffs. Whenever the coach was asked about him, the reply was: "Jim's not ready yet—he doesn't know the plays well enough." Then, in the last two games of the season, the coach decided to give Taylor a chance, and the rookie made good his opportunity. After looking at the films of those games, Lombardi was convinced that Taylor would be a dependable fullback.

Though Hornung and Taylor were to be key figures in Packer comeback plans, Lombardi depended equally on his offensive and defensive lines. His blockers included center Jim Ringo, guards Fred "Fuzzy" Thurston and Jerry Kramer, and tackles Forrest Gregg and Bob Skoronski, with Norm Masters in reserve at tackle.

One of Lombardi's tasks was to make his blockers believe they were the best around, for some of them had developed inferiority complexes. Thurston had been discarded four times by league teams—twice by Philadelphia and by the Bears and Colts once. Masters had been drafted by the Cardinals and traded to the Lions, but he had never played for either team before being sent on to the Packers. The defensive forward wall included Jordan and Bill Quinlan, two men who had played with the Cleveland Browns before being shipped on. Other defensive players were lineman Dave Hanner; linebackers Forester, Dan Currie, Ray Nitschke and Tom Bettis; defensive backs Jesse Whittenton, Gremminger, Emlen Tunnell, John Symank, Willie Wood and Herb Adderley.

The only real problem spot for Lombardi was quarterback. The coach was not sure whether to play Starr or Lamar McHan. Finally he decided on McHan, who played quarterback until midseason, when he was injured. Starr took advantage of his absence, and played well enough to keep McHan out of the line-up even when he was healthy again. With Starr at the helm during the last half of the 1959 season, the Packers wound up with a record of seven wins and five losses, and tied for third place in the Western Conference.

Lombardi's methods had paid off in his first season. The Packers had become a respectable team once again. Lombardi's faith in Hornung and Taylor had been borne out, too. Hornung had gained 681 yards on the ground for seven touchdowns; completed five of eight passes for 95 yards and two touchdowns; kicked 17 field goals and 31 extra points. Taylor had rushed for 452 yards and six touchdowns. Still, there was plenty of room for improvement.

At the end of the season, Lombardi adjusted his offense slightly. He installed a system using three ends. He explained his decision by saying, "I do not like the three-end system of offense. I prefer a system with three running backs. But we use the three-end system because it is better suited to our present personnel."

Those personnel included two fine sets of ends. Max McGee, Boyd Dowler and Gary Knafelc were the regulars, with Ron Kramer, Steve Meilinger and Lew Carpenter as the reserves.

When the 1960 season began, Lombardi still had not made up his mind about his quarterbacks. Starr was learning, but the coach did not think he could do the job as well as McHan. So McHan opened the season as the starting quarterback. Once again, though, Starr came off the bench to replace him, and performed well. In fact, he did so well that the Packers compiled a record of eight wins, four losses, and won the Western Conference title.

It was as remarkable a turnabout as any team

had achieved in just two seasons. But for Lombardi it was spoiled by Green Bay's 17-13 loss to the Philadelphia Eagles in the NFL title game. More than anything else he wanted the Packers to be acclaimed as the best team in pro football. He would not rest until he had attained that goal.

When the 1961 training season started, the Packers appeared even stronger than they had been the year before. They had added Willie Davis, a defensive end, to their already tough front four. Davis, like Jordan and Quinlan, had come to Green Bay from Cleveland. Lombardi convinced him that the Browns had made a mistake in letting him go. The coach seemed to work magic on other teams' rejects.

That season one of Lombardi's own rejects, tight end Ron Kramer, came into his own. Kramer had been benched the year before when he got his signals crossed on a pass play and had cut the wrong way. But in preseason practice in 1961, he hit his teammates so hard that Lombardi pardoned his past sins and made him a first stringer.

Even though he had a high caliber team now, Lombardi was just as tough as he had been in the first training camp. He still played no favorites. Anybody could be the target of his displeasure. For instance, at one point during the 1961 training session, the Packers were running a two-one-one drill. Taylor was the ball carrier, Nitschke was the tackler, and a 265-pound rookie was assigned to block Nitschke. The action was confined within two blocking dummies and, with so little running room, the blocker merely had to place himself in Nitschke's way while Taylor slid by. Lombardi stopped the drill after the first play. He said, "Mr. Nitschke, I have read that you are the best linebacker in the NFL, and after watching you just then, I find that difficult to believe. Do it again."

This time Nitschke grabbed the rookie by the shoulder pads, literally lifted him up and threw him into Taylor. All Lombardi said was, "Next group." The unfortunate rookie did not wake up for two minutes.

Throughout camp Lombardi nagged the Packers, reminding them how close they'd come to the championship. He told them that they could still be the best team in the NFL and that he didn't expect them to fail this season.

Lombardi's encouragement seemed to have little effect, however, for in Green Bay's opening game the Detroit Lions upset the defending Western Conference champions, 17-13. Although the Packers gained a total of 305 yards that Sunday, they were unable to score crucial points.

What hurt more was the way the Lions scored their winning touchdown. Quinlan rushed Detroit quarterback Earl Morrall so hard that Morrall resorted to a "safety-valve" pass (thrown to a back-

Paul Hornung kicks a field goal during the Packers'

game with the Lions.

field player behind the line of scrimmage and near the sideline) to fullback Nick Pietrosante. This kind of play is generally a short-gainer. Not this time, however. Pietrosante went 15 yards for the touchdown.

The Packers were shaken by the defeat, and they did not need Lombardi's goading to prepare themselves for their next opponent, the San Francisco 49ers. Green Bay scored the first time it got the ball, and kept on scoring. Starr, now a first stringer, completed 11 of 16 passes for 161 yards and a touchdown. Hornung gained 51 yards rushing, kicked three field goals and scored a touchdown. Taylor contributed 63 yards rushing. The Packers won, 30-10. Lombardi's men had regained their confidence.

Against the Chicago Bears the following week, the defense intercepted four passes which Starr and his offensive teammates quickly converted to points. Starr, growing more assured as a starter, threw an 18-yard touchdown pass to Boyd Dowler and later connected with a 17-yard touchdown pass to end Kramer, who was remembering plays now. In between Starr's two touchdown passes, Taylor scored from three yards out and Hornung kicked a 37-yard field goal. The score was Green Bay 24, Chicago 0.

Baltimore was next, and if any team in the Western Conference was capable of preventing another Packer victory it was Johnny Unitas and company. The game was billed as a battle between two NFL giants, but by the time Paul Hornung was finished, the excitement appeared rather silly. The Packer halfback gave a brilliant exhibition of his ability "to find daylight." The first time he got the ball, he started to run to his left, then cut into the heart of the Colt secondary and raced 54 yards for the touchdown. "The Golden Boy" scored a total of four touchdowns, kicked six extra points and a field goal, thereby contributing 33 points to Green Bay's lopsided 45-7 victory.

Although Hornung was the star that afternoon, Green Bay's defense was responsible for the play that most experts considered the turning point of the game. The Packers had only a slim lead (10-7) when Unitas tried to hit end Ray Berry with a pass. However, Whittenton, the Packers' right cornerback, intercepted. From then on, Hornung and the Green Bay offense took over.

Against Cleveland the next week, Hornung took a back seat to Taylor. Prior to the game, the Packer fullback had heard glowing reports on the ability of the Browns' fullback, Jim Brown. By Sunday he was ready to dispute those reports. Taylor outgained Brown, 158 yards to 72, and contributed four touchdowns to Green Bay's victory over Cleveland, 49-17.

When Taylor wasn't gaining yardage against

the Browns on the ground, Starr was passing. The 27-year-old quarterback completed 15 of his 17 passes for 271 yards and a 48-yard touchdown pass to Max McGee. With each week, Lombardi was wondering why he had ever doubted Starr's capacity to lead the team.

Against Minnesota, it was Hornung's turn to star, at least until he injured his knee. Up to that point, he kicked field goals of 14, 18, 13 and 16 yards. After he left the game, the Packers discovered that his absence did not hurt them as much as they had expected. Hornung's replacement, Tom Moore,

Hornung breaks through Viking defenses for a long gain.

Jim Taylor prepares to meet the charge of a Viking defender.

ran 69 yards for a touchdown. Once again, though, the Packer defense did its share in sealing the victory. Three times Green Bay interceptions crushed Viking drives. On one of those plays, linebacker Currie carried the interception 21 yards for the touchdown. The final score was 33-7.

Seven days later, Minnesota had a chance to avenge its loss. But again Hornung stopped the Vikings. He put the Packers in the lead by scoring after a 67-yard drive from Green Bay's own one. Shortly afterwards, he threw a 10-yard option pass to Kramer. From then on Starr's leadership carried the team to another victory. He completed 18 of 24 passes for 311 yards and two touchdowns, one scored on a 10-yard pass to Taylor and the other on a 22-yard pass to McGee. The score for the return match was Green Bay 28, Minnesota 10.

But the victory was costly. Blocking guard Jerry Kramer had fractured a small bone above his left ankle, end Ron Kramer had a badly sprained ankle and Hornung a pinched nerve. For Hornung and Ron Kramer, the injuries were not serious, but Jerry Kramer was finished for the season.

For Lombardi, the biggest blow was the news that the government had activated linebacker Nitschke's military reserve unit as a result of the "Berlin crisis" (caused by the Soviet Union's demand that the United States and its allies withdraw from the city and by the erection of the "Berlin Wall"). Even though the Packers had a six-game winning streak, Lombardi did not like the idea of facing the revenge-minded Colts the following week with injured personnel and without Nitschke.

As it turned out, Nitschke's loss was confined merely to the week's practice sessions. That weekend he received a pass that enabled him to play for Green Bay. (Because of weekend passes he missed only two games that season.) Still, Lombardi knew that, without practice, Nitschke's timing would suffer and, ultimately, Green Bay would suffer, too—especially against the Colts.

Lombardi was right. The next Sunday, Unitas, smarting from the 45-7 defeat earlier in the season, evened the score. He threw for four touchdowns and Baltimore won, 45-21. Fortunately, the defeat of the Chicago Bears kept Green Bay in first place by a game.

Chicago was the Packers' next foe, and they knew the Bears would be fighting for a first-place tie in the Western Conference. Hornung played an outstanding game and scored 19 points, including a 51-yard field goal. Chicago, trailing 31-7, tried hard to recover, and nearly succeeded. But Hornung's field goal proved to be the winning margin in the Packers' 31-28 victory. After the game, Hornung departed for Ft. Riley, Kansas. Like Nitschke, he had been reactivated by the Army during crisis times.

Lombardi, naturally, was not pleased to see another of his players become unavailable, especially when that player was his top offensive threat. Still, he did not panic. "The loss of this many regulars, even on a part-time basis, would hurt any team," Lombardi said. "But if there is a team which can overcome such adversity, the Packers are the team. They have great confidence in themselves, individually and as a team. They believe in themselves."

The coach's praise was justified. The following week, without Hornung, the Packers beat the Los

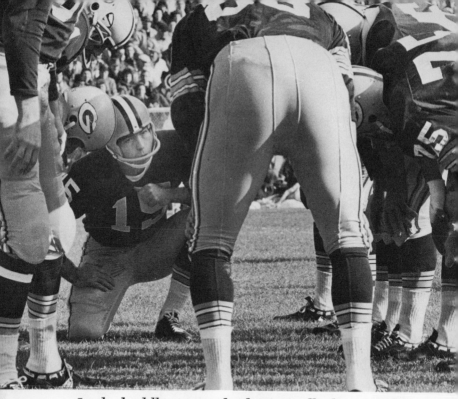

In the huddle, quarterback Starr calls the next play.

Angeles Rams, 35-17. Starr more than made up for Hornung's absence. He completed 10 of 15 passes for 173 yards and three touchdowns. Mc-Gee caught two of them and Dowler caught the other.

Detroit was now the biggest threat in the Western Conference, trailing the Packers by only a game-and-a-half. The Lions had a chance to cut that lead when they met Green Bay the following Sunday. Hornung was back for the game, having obtained a weekend pass, and he contributed a nine-yard field goal. But Taylor was even more effective. He scored two touchdowns, and Green Bay won, 17-9.

Again, the Green Bay defense had brought about the turning point of the game. The Packers had been trailing, 9-7, when defensive back Adderley intercepted a pass and returned it 40 yards. His interception set up the winning score for the Packers.

The Packer defense also turned the tide against the New York Giants. Green Bay was behind, 17-13, in the fourth quarter when Whittenton stole the ball from Alex Webster. Five plays later, Taylor scored. The touchdown highlighted a big day for Taylor. On 27 carries, he had gained 186 yards and scored two touchdowns.

The victory gave the Packers their second straight Western Conference title, though they still had two games left to play on their schedule. In the afterglow of victory, Lombardi reminded them, "This was a good victory, but let's remember we still have a job to do."

The Packers split their last two games by losing to San Francisco, 22-21, and beating Los Angeles, 24-17. Then they began to get ready for the New York Giants, who had won in ence. One break was the ava Because he'd gotten a pass for would have a chance to pick more important, the coordinati the previous seven weeks. Nitschke also received special permission to leave his military duties to play in the title game.

The game was to be played in Green Bay, and the little town quite naturally was excited. Before the arrival of Coach Lombardi, few people in Green Bay would have expected an NFL title game to be played there.

The Giants were working out in cold weather in New York, but it was nothing like winter in Green Bay. On the Tuesday before the game, the temperature dropped to 12 below zero in Green Bay. It was unpleasant weather for playing football, but the Giants were coming prepared. Their equipment trunks contained, among other things, basketball shoes, gloves, scarves and protective ponchos. As game day neared, it appeared that all their equipment and more would be needed for the cold. The winds charged down Green Bay's narrow streets and temperatures hovered around the zero mark. It was, natives agreed, perfect football weather.

The Giants arrived on Thursday, and by the time their plane landed, the weather had warmed to a relatively balmy 15 degrees. The excitement in Green Bay was growing. All over town, storefront signs urged the Packers to beat the Giants. one of the hotels visitors would roll over in bed swer the phone and hear the desk clerk say,

"Howdy, Packer-backer. It's eight o'clock."

On game day, a record crowd of 39,029 people jammed into Green Bay City Stadium. Since it was the first title game ever played in Green Bay, tickets were extremely scarce. Those who couldn't get into the ballpark relied on their radios.

Early in the game, New York coach Allie Sherman installed an odd, five-man line. It worked briefly, until Starr sent Hornung racing easily through the strong side of the Packer line behind the blocking of Ron Kramer, Ringo, Skoronski and Gregg. The Giants went back to their normal defense, but it didn't matter to the Packers, who simply knocked down anyone in sight. But the Giants hung on. At the end of the first quarter, the score was still 0-0.

In the second quarter, the Packers picked up more momentum. This time the Giants could not stop them. Green Bay drove 74 yards in 10 plays, and then Hornung scored from the six. The off-tackle play that the Packers liked to use to crush the spirit of a defense was working. To make sure that linebacker Sam Huff couldn't swing wide to make the tackles, Ringo would brush-block him, then Jerry Kramer would cross over to hit him.

Less than five minutes after the first score, Nitschke intercepted a pass by Giant quarterback Y. A. Tittle that was tipped by Jordan. With the ball on the New York 33, Green Bay started another scoring drive. After two passes had failed, Starr completed one to Ron Kramer at the 17. Taylor gained four yards in two carries. Then Starr hit Dowler in the deep right flat (the flat is any area of the playing field behind an offensive end) with a 13-yard touchdown pass.

Green Bay was not finished for the first half. Once again the Packer defense got the ball. This time Gremminger intercepted at the New York 36. Hornung and Taylor punched out first downs on the 25 and 15. Taylor picked up another yard. Then Starr passed to Ron Kramer, who went 14 yards for the touchdown.

The play Starr had called was known as the "flood-right pass." It was designed to trick the middle linebacker (in this case, Huff) into moving to his left to help his teammates handle the flood of potential receivers on that side. Kramer, playing tight end on the right side, blocked hard on the corner linebacker in front of him, creating the impression that he wasn't a pass receiver. Then, with the flow of receivers moving to the right, Kramer caught the ball in the territory Huff had vacated and was able to score unmolested.

Kramer's touchdown broke the spirit of the Giants. Before the first half ended Hornung added a field goal to make the score, 24-0. After the half-time intermission he resumed the Packer attack with another field goal. The next time Green Bay

Guard Fuzzy Thurston (63) runs interference for Hornung during the 1961 title game.

got the ball, Kramer faked the flood-right pass pattern over the center and broke to the outside. Although New York's Joe Morrison covered him well, Kramer caught Starr's pass for a 13-yard touchdown. Then Hornung kicked his third field goal. The Packers won, 37-0.

It was a beautiful exhibition of Lombardi-style football. With basic knockdown tactics, the Packers had battered New York into submission. It was the same Giant team that had nearly beaten Green Bay earlier in the season, losing only when the Packers managed a late interception. But Green Bay had been driven by the memory of how close they had come to the NFL title the year before. They had no intention of allowing the 1961 title game to be close. The rejects and has-beens were now the champions of the NFL.

"Here's something," said Jim Ringo afterwards. "Nine of the guys on our offensive starting team in the championship game also started when we lost our tenth game in 1958. Vince made a lot of boys into men. He tells us you have to be dedicated. That's what he is. . . . He makes you feel your responsibility as a football player."

Forester put it another way: "The Giants were more concerned about the weather than anything else. They brought all kinds of things to keep them warm. We weren't worried about the weather. We just came to play."

For their performance the Packers won the ultimate praise—that is, Lombardi's praise. He said very simply: "There has never been a better team than this one was today."

CLEVELAND
BROWNS
1964

It was discouraging to be a member of the Cleveland Browns in the early 1960s. The days of glory—when the team had had such players as Otto Graham, Marion Motley, Dub Jones and Dante Lavelli—had apparently vanished. From 1950 through 1955 the Browns had won six straight division crowns and three NFL championships. Cleveland's coach, Paul Brown, seemed to have a magic touch because everything he put his football mind to became a success.

Unfortunately, Cleveland had not won a conference title since 1957 or an NFL championship since 1955. By 1962 the people who played football for Paul Brown were grumbling. Mainly, they were grumbling about Brown. Bob August, sports editor of the Cleveland *Press*, explained the problem this way:

Without the championships to smooth their feelings, the players have grown resentful of the tight discipline [of Paul Brown]. They question the play-calling [Brown called every play]. They resent the popular conception of them as puppets with Paul Brown pulling the strings. Players have talked privately about quitting. It has become questionable whether the Brown system can remain in operation without yielding a large annual dividend in victories. It was not made for mediocrity.

Understandably, their viewpoint is different from that of the players with whom the original team was built in 1946. Most of these had been through the war. They came back broke and unsettled and conscious of the time they had lost. Some, like Dante Lavelli and Lou Groza, had not had a chance to establish themselves as college stars before entering the service. They were looking for a chance, and they were, in one of Brown's favorite phrases, "willing to pay the price" of football success.

Players arriving in recent years also are willing to pay the price, but they are haggling over whether it has to be as high as the one Brown would exact. They have been sought after and fought over by the two rival American leagues and Canada. Their starting pay is higher than an established pro could realize 10 years ago.

They are not burdened by the economic pressures that spurred on the early Browns.

Whatever their reasons, the Cleveland players just did not like Paul Brown. That might not have bothered anybody if, as August suggested, the Browns had kept on winning. But it became increasingly clear that the players could not win for Brown any more. So the team's owner, Art Modell, fired Paul Brown at the end of the 1962 season. Cleveland had finished third in the Eastern Conference with a mediocre record of seven wins, six losses and one tie.

The players were not disappointed to see Brown go. Jim Brown, the star Cleveland fullback, said, "I feel Modell had good reason to fire Brown. Football players don't like to be treated as inferiors."

Said Bernie Parrish, defensive back and player representative: "I checked with my teammates, and I'm virtually certain they were 100 percent in favor of the change."

Cleveland named one of Paul Brown's assistants, Blanton Collier, the new head coach, but the team's trouble did not end at that point. People just couldn't take the Browns seriously any more —and maybe with good reason. In Collier's first season, Cleveland won its first six games, then faded badly to finish second with a record of 10 victories and four losses. There was a suspicion

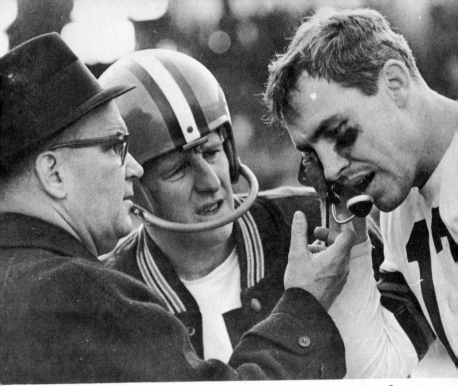

Coach Collier and quarterback Frank Ryan (with the field telephone).

among football experts that the Browns didn't have the necessary spirit to win the important games.

There was also harsh criticism of individual players, and the doubts increased as the 1964 season began. The experts saw the defensive line as a patchwork of fading veterans—Bill Glass, Paul Wiggin, Frank Parker, Dick Modzelewski, who had been traded to Cleveland from New York—and an inexperienced youngster named Jim Kanicki. The defensive secondary was not considered tall enough to deal with the NFL's rangy pass catchers. Quarterback Frank Ryan, a prematurely graying man with a genius' IQ, was regarded as too inconsistent to lead the Browns to a championship.

Not even the great Jim Brown was exempt from criticism. There had always been a feeling among some football people that Brown was not a complete football player. Brown was for Brown only, according to their thinking. He was a fine runner, but he would never block for others, they said. This opinion became more than just gossip in NFL inner circles when former Cleveland quarterback, Otto Graham, said in public: "If I were the Browns' coach, I would tell the fullback [Brown] I would trade him if he didn't block and fake." Graham went on to say that the Browns could not win a title as long as Jim Brown was their starting fullback.

The Browns read the newspapers, of course, so they knew what was said about them. Although they would have liked to ignore the barbed remarks, they couldn't. Since they were professionals, they had pride in their work. Nor could they ignore the fact that they had lost their opportunity to win the Eastern Conference title the year before—that was history. So, with their past performances in mind, the Browns vowed to make their critics change their minds by winning everything in 1964.

Winning an NFL championship is never easy.

But in the Browns' case, the difficulties were compounded by the self-doubt caused by their disastrous finish the season before. Collier knew what the players were thinking. Before the season began, he told them: "I ask you to forget last year, except for correcting mistakes. People remember the games that are badly played. We've got the players to do the job. Let's get out there and do it."

The players who would have to do the job were mostly men who hadn't been able to win under Paul Brown. On the offensive line were ends Gary Collins and John Brewer, tackles John Brown and Dick Schafrath, guards John Wooten and Gene Hickerson and center John Morrow. In the backfield were quarterback Ryan, running backs Ernie Green, Jim Brown and flanker Paul Warfield. The defensive forward wall was comprised of Glass, Wiggin, Parker or Modzelewski, and Kanicki. The linebackers were Vince Costello, Galen Fiss and Jim Houston. Cleveland's defensive secondary included Parrish, Walter Beach, Larry Benz and Ross Fichtner. Of these players, only Warfield, Kanicki, Beach and Benz had not played under Paul Brown. The rest had, and they especially wanted to prove they were winners.

But in the opening game against Washington, it seemed as if the Browns were picking up where they'd left off the previous season. Moments after the kickoff, a pass from Ryan was intercepted by

Redskin rookie Paul Krause. And two plays later another rookie, Charley Taylor, scampered 17 yards for a touchdown. Early in the second quarter, Washington widened the gap by three more points on Jim Martin's 12-yard field goal.

Then Cleveland began to take advantage of their opponent's mistakes, an ability the team demonstrated throughout the season, causing some people to call the Browns lucky. Mike Lucci pounced on the Redskins' fumble of Collins' punt, and Ryan followed with a touchdown pass to Collins in the end zone. With less than three minutes of the half remaining, Jim Brown burst through from the one to give the Browns a 13-10 lead.

The first half also brought misfortune to Cleveland. Frank Parker, the Browns' defensive right tackle, injured his left knee and was all but finished for the season. Modzelewski replaced Parker in the second half, and with "Little Mo" leading the defensive charge, the Redskin attack bogged down. The Browns, meanwhile, capitalized on another Redskin mishap when Beach recovered a fumble by flankerback Bobby Mitchell. A 32-yard pass from Ryan to Ernie Green brought the ball to the one. Then Brown scored again to make the score, 20-10. The final tally was 27-13.

After the game, the Browns voted to give the game ball to Modzelewski. Said Little Mo: "It's my first game ball in twelve years as a pro. The

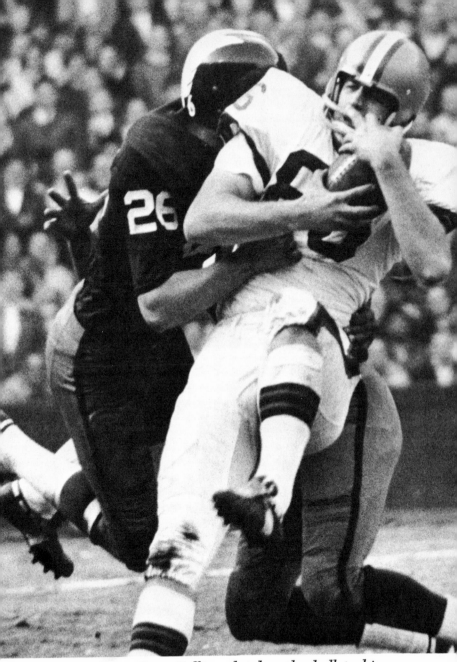

Pass receiver Gary Collins clutches the ball to his chest as Redskin defenders crash into him.

Giants never gave them to the slobs on the line."
Modzelewski was not the only star that afternoon.
Brown had rushed for 89 yards, almost as much as
the Redskins' total rushing yardage of 96 yards.
And Ryan had completed 17 of 30 passes, one of
them for a touchdown.

The next game was one of the most exciting of
the year for the Browns. With less than a minute-
and-a-half left in the game, they trailed the St.
Louis (formerly Chicago) Cardinals, 30-26. In
addition, they were in a fourth-down-and-19-yards-
to-go predicament on St. Louis' 45-yard line.

Coach Blanton Collier sent rookie Clifton Mc-
Neil into the game with a play. But Ryan waved
him off the field. He had his own idea. Collier was
no Paul Brown; he had faith in his players. So he
stood along the sidelines and waited to see what
his quarterback would do. Ryan's plan was to send
Collins deep.

Gary faked to the outside and then headed for
the goal posts. Two St. Louis defenders went up
into the air with him, but the Cleveland end came
down with the ball on the St. Louis two-yard line.
Two plays later, with 48 seconds remaining in the
game, Jim Brown swept to the right side for a
touchdown. After kicking the extra point, the
Browns led, 33-30.

Then Cleveland went into a "prevent" defense. (This is an arrangement designed to guard

Ryan calls signals during the game with the Cardinals.

against a long pass that could lead to a touchdown. The short pass is conceded to the offensive team.) A tackle departed from the line and Mike Lucci moved in as an extra linebacker. Cardinal quarterback Charley Johnson threw to fullback Joe Childress for 24 yards. Moments later he hit Sonny

Randle for 14 yards. Then Johnson found John David Crow in the open and connected with a pass that was good for 16 yards. The ball was on the Cleveland 21, with 11 seconds remaining. Into the game came Cardinal place kicker Jim Baaken to boot the field goal that tied the game, 33-33.

Although Cleveland had to settle for the tie, it was a satisfying game for the team. The Browns had come through with a big play in the clutch. They were proving to themselves and their critics that the Browns were a championship ball club. Ryan appeared to be finding the consistency he had been faulted for previously. He had completed 12 of 26 passes for 166 yards and two touchdowns. Brown made blocking seem unimportant: he had gained 79 yards in 21 carries.

In their next game, against Philadelphia, the Browns continued to show the kind of spunk the experts had thought they lacked. Although they trailed, 13-7, at half time, Ryan and his teammates picked up momentum in the last half. Ryan, who had completed only three of 11 passes before the intermission, threw a 24-yard touchdown pass to Warfield in the third period. Then, four minutes later, he hit Brown with a 40-yard touchdown pass. In the fourth quarter, he completed a 12-yard touchdown pass to Collins.

Warfield and Brown also sparked the Cleveland offense in that game. Warfield caught six passes for 97 yards; Brown gained 103 yards on the ground and 53 yards on passes. But the defense did its part, too. The Browns recovered two fumbles and intercepted a pass, continuing to take advantage of every opportunity. (In their first three games, they had recovered eight of eight fumbles.) The final score was 28-20.

Against Dallas the following week, Cleveland didn't have to come from behind. Although the Cowboys staged the first scoring threat of the game, their field-goal attempt by Dick Van Raaphorst was blocked. Then the Browns concluded a scoring march with a seven-yard pass from Ryan to Green. During this drive, a screen pass (a short pass over oncharging linemen who are intentionally missed by blockers) accounted for 41 yards.

Lou Groza, the veteran place kicker, continued the Cleveland attack with two field goals in the second period. At the half Cleveland led, 13-6. Near the end of the third period, Ryan gave Cleveland a 20-6 lead by tossing a 40-yard pass to Warfield in the end zone. The Browns' final score came in the fourth period on a 38-yard pass from Ryan to Gary Collins. The final score was 27-6.

Ryan's performance was his finest of the season up to that point. He had completed 15 passes in 26 attempts for 256 yards and three touchdowns. In the last four games he had thrown a total of nine touchdown passes.

Collins also distinguished himself, for it was the sixth straight game in which he caught one or more touchdown passes (three of the games were played in 1963). He cracked the old club mark of five set by Dante Lavelli in 1954 and equaled by Ray Renfro in 1955-1956.

Along with the pleasure of victory, however, the game brought certain costs. Offensive tackle Bob Gain sustained a fractured leg which sidelined him the rest of the year, and safetyman Ross Fichtner was carried off with a serious concussion that kept him out of action until the final two games.

Once again the Browns were off to a good start. They had won four games in a row, and they had done so in a convincing manner. Ryan had been in consistently good form, and Brown had been running in superb style—and even blocking a little. And there were no complaints about the so-called lucky defense. Then the Browns met the Pittsburgh Steelers.

The Steelers' fullback was named John Henry Johnson. That afternoon he set a career high and a club record as he rushed for 200 yards. He also scored three touchdowns, and Pittsburgh upset the Browns, 23-7.

The Steelers made the defeat more embarrassing by playing without linebackers Bob Schmitz and Bob Harrison, both of whom had knee injuries. To make up for their loss, coach Buddy Parker used an unorthodox six-man line. The strategy worked. Jim Brown's rushing was limited to 59 yards and Ryan was rendered ineffective as a passer. Afterwards Collier said, "We were beaten in just about every way you can lose."

Said John Henry Johnson, "I just started running and nobody stopped me."

Fortunately, Cleveland remained tied for first place with St. Louis when the Cardinals also lost. A return game with Dallas was next, and the Browns knew they had to win to avoid the possibility of another slide after a good start. This game

Lanky Clifton McNeil makes an attempt to catch one of Ryan's passes in the Steeler end zone. A moment later he dropped the ball.

was one of Cleveland's most courageous efforts of 1964. Defensive halfback Bernie Parrish emerged as the hero in a dramatic play that matched in importance the Ryan-Collins pass of the St. Louis game. Since two of the Browns' regular defensive backs, Benz and Fichtner, were sidelined by injuries, Parrish had quite a job trying to prevent Cowboy quarterback Don Meredith from exploiting the weakened secondary.

With only six minutes remaining in the game, the Browns trailed, 16-13. Dallas had the ball on its own 23. Meredith, attempting to surprise the Browns at this point, lofted a long, high pass intended for Frank Clarke. But Parrish moved in and leaped high to grab it. He raced 54 yards with the interception for the winning touchdown.

Parrish wasn't the only hero in that game. Brown gained 188 yards rushing for his finest day of the season up to that point. And even though Collins' touchdown-catching streak was stopped at seven games, he had the satisfaction of preventing a Dallas touchdown by tackling speedy Mel Renfro after a 51-yard return of Collins' own punt.

Toward the end of the Dallas game, there was some added excitement when Cowboy defensive end George Andrie roughed up Ryan. Fullback Brown went after Andrie, and before the scrap had gone very far some Cleveland fans spilled onto the field. The police had to step in to avoid a riot.

Ryan was being knocked around in other ways, too. After the Dallas game, Cleveland fans began calling for reserve quarterback Jim Ninowski. The game had resulted in the second straight bad effort for Ryan. He had completed only nine passes for 95 yards. But Collier remained calm. "There's no cause for the panic button," he said. "There is no need to blame Ryan any more than all of us for the offensive difficulties. Everybody was at fault."

The next game was more encouraging. Going into the last quarter, the Browns were behind, 14-13, but their knack of making their own breaks led to a 28-point final quarter. Within the span of four-and-a-half minutes, they scored three touchdowns as a result of two fumble recoveries and an interception.

They received their first break when New York's Dick James fumbled at the three and defensive end Paul Wiggin scooped up the ball on the two and went into the end zone for the score. Next, Cleveland linebacker Jim Houston intercepted a pass by Y. A. Tittle that had bounced off the shoulder of rookie halfback Steve Thurlow. Houston returned the interception 44 yards to the New York 31. Then Ryan threw to Collins for nine yards and a touchdown. Clarence Childs of the Giants fumbled the next kickoff on his 23 and Charley Scales picked the ball up and returned it for a touchdown.

Later in the period, the Browns scored their

fourth touchdown of the quarter when Jim Ninowski passed 11 yards to Brewer. Cleveland won,
42-20. It had been a great day for the defense. Surprisingly, the same players had been considered
a weak link in the Browns' game.

The victory, coupled with St. Louis' loss to Dallas, gave the Browns sole possession of first place.
The following week, Cleveland met the Steelers
again. Collins was sidelined by a pulled ham-
string muscle and Warfield was handicapped by a
similar injury, which severely limited the Browns'
scoring ability. But Lou Groza kicked a field goal
in the second period to put Cleveland on the scoreboard. Shortly afterwards, Ryan threw to Clifton
McNeil, Collins' replacement, for a 25-yard touchdown. At half time the score was 10-10.

Benz's second interception of the game set up a
Cleveland touchdown early in the third period.
Green put the Browns ahead, 17-10, when he
scored on a seven-yard drive over tackle. The
Browns went on to win, 30-17.

Brown and Green had teamed up for Cleveland's finest running effort of the year. Brown
gained 149 yards, Green added 86. The victory
avenged the earlier loss to the Steelers. And it was
particularly important because the second-place
Cardinals were upset by New York, thus giving
Cleveland a two-game lead.

The Browns held that lead by beating Washington the following week. Again, they had to come from behind to win. Washington scored first when Jim Martin kicked a 30-yard field goal early in the second period. But this time the Browns did not trail for long. Green caught a pass from Ryan and ran 21 yards for a touchdown. Then, despite a fractured nose received earlier in the period, Groza kicked two field goals.

After half-time rest, Cleveland kept scoring. In the third period, Brown started to his right, suddenly stopped and threw the ball. Collins caught Brown's only pass of the season for a 13-yard touchdown. Cleveland won, 34-24.

Detroit was next on Cleveland's schedule. By the half, the Browns were trailing, 21-10. Then, as it had done so many times that season, the team asserted itself after intermission. Detroit never threatened in the last half, and the Browns' surprising defense held the Lions to only four first downs. Ryan's pass for eight yards to Warfield put the Browns ahead in the third period. Then, with less than two minutes of play remaining in the game, Groza's 36-yard field goal put victory out of reach for the Lions. On top of that, as the final gun sounded, defensive back Beach intercepted a Detroit pass and ran 65 yards for his first touchdown in the NFL. Cleveland 37, Detroit 21.

By winning, the Browns increased their lead over the Cardinals, who were tied by New York

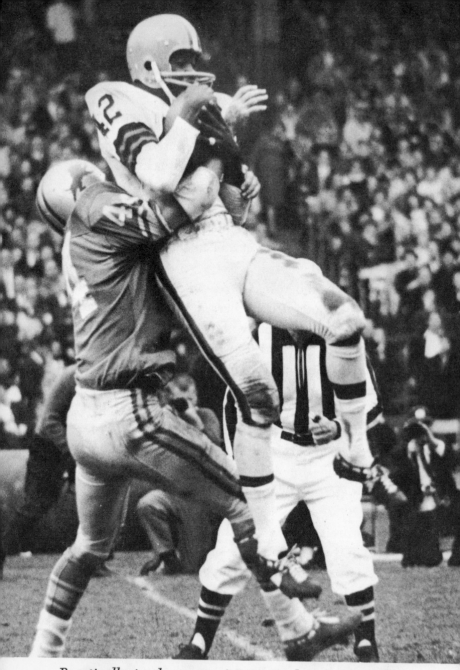

*Practically in the arms of Lion Dick LeBeau, Paul
Warfield catches a pass from Ryan.*

that weekend. With four games to go, the Browns had a two-and-a-half-game margin. But they weren't overconfident. In the backs of their minds, they had the memories of their collapse in 1963.

And after their experience with Green Bay the following week, some of the players must have wondered if history would repeat itself. This time, Cleveland was the victim of interceptions and fumbles. The score was 14-14 when Green Bay recovered a fumble on the Cleveland 22, and then scored on a "keeper" play by Bart Starr. (A keeper is a play in which the quarterback maintains possession of the ball and runs with it, usually toward the sidelines.) A Cleveland scoring threat was halted by Dan Currie's interception on the Packers' 26. Jim Taylor's second touchdown of the day increased the Packers' lead to 28-14. Ryan's second touchdown pass of the game to Warfield narrowed the gap, but a fumble and an interception halted Cleveland's attack. The final score, Green Bay 28, Cleveland 21.

Meanwhile, St. Louis defeated Philadelphia to cut Cleveland's lead to a game-and-a-half, and Brown fans crossed their fingers and hoped that their team would get back to their winning ways when they met the Philadelphia Eagles the next week.

On the opening kickoff, Cleveland's previously maligned defenders began to redeem themselves

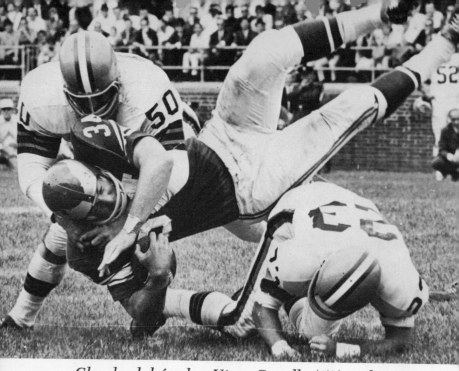

Cleveland defenders Vince Costello (50) and Larry Benz (23) team up to stop Earl Gros during the game with the Eagles.

by jarring the football loose from Eagle halfback Tim Brown. The ball bounced backward toward the goal line as both teams tried to recover it. Several of the Browns had a chance to stop the elusive pigskin, but missed. Finally, Roger Shoals landed on the ball just inside the end zone for a Cleveland touchdown.

In the second period, the defense kept up the pressure. Sidney Williams blocked and recovered Sam Baker's kick in the end zone to give Cleveland its second touchdown. Houston's 44-yard return of an intercepted pass gave the Browns a 21-3 half-time lead. In the last half, Ryan threw two touchdown passes to Brewer. Cleveland won by a score of 38-24.

Cleveland played the St. Louis Cardinals next, and needed either a victory or a tie to give them the Eastern Conference title. They got neither, however, for St. Louis broke the game open in the second period with 21 points and went on to win, 28-19. The season had come down to the final contest, and St. Louis now trailed Cleveland by only half a game.

The Browns faced a difficult task. Their last opponents would be the defending Eastern Conference champions, the New York Giants. The Browns knew that the sporting world would accuse them of failing under pressure if they lost this game. And for professional athletes there is no worse charge. But after the Browns finished with the Giants, nobody could reasonably suggest that they were unable to stand up under pressure.

During the game Ryan was thoroughly consistent. He hit on 12 of 13 passes for 202 yards and five touchdowns. The final score was 52-20. Even the New York writer who had called the Browns the "laugh champs" because they often received lucky breaks had to change his mind. To his readers he finally admitted the Browns had come through in the clutch.

Despite that, some people still did not take the

Despite an apparent fumble, Ryan scores Cleveland's first touchdown as he falls into New York's end zone.

Browns very seriously. Cleveland was the champion of the Eastern Conference, but to so-called football experts that wasn't much of an achievement. According to them, Baltimore—the Western Conference winner—was certain to win the NFL title. Even before Cleveland had won in the East, Edwin Shrake had written in *Sports Illustrated:*

This year it is yawningly conceded that the Eastern champion—probably Cleveland—will be playing merely for the dubious pleasure of being thrashed by Baltimore on December 27. There are at least three teams in the West that are superior to any in the East. To be realistic about it, the championship game of 1964 already has been played. Baltimore won it in October by beating Green Bay for the second time.

The Browns were used to reading stories criticizing the team. Before the 1964 season, a number of writers had said they couldn't win the crucial ball games. Well, the Browns had won the Eastern Conference championship, and now the same writers were saying that Cleveland didn't have a chance against Baltimore. What the press said about individual players was especially painful. Most sportswriters gave the impression that the Browns were overmatched at almost every position. Unitas was better than Ryan, Berry was better than Collins, etc. That kind of writing was bound to arouse the Browns.

In tackle Jim Kanicki's case, it was more than what the writers said. His own neighbors had started to kid him. A few days before the game, Kanicki was pushing his cart through a supermarket in his town when the store manager asked:

"Hey, you gonna show up for that game Sunday? I just read a magazine article that says the Colts are gonna run at you every time they need five yards."

It was true that Kanicki, the youngest member of Cleveland's defensive front four, was the most vulnerable, but he had learned with each game. He didn't like to be considered a pushover. Against Baltimore, he would be playing opposite Jim Parker, the 275-pound All-NFL tackle. "It is unreasonable to assume that he [Kanicki] will be able to defeat an All-League guard like Parker," said *Sports Illustrated*.

Kanicki was determined not to be cowed by the criticism and vowed to play the game of his life.

Other Cleveland players, including Ryan, Collins, Brown and Modzelewski, were equally determined. It was time to make people recognize that the Browns were no laugh champs, but the best team in professional football.

The week before the game, the Browns worked hard in practice. And after practice, they studied their notes on the Colts and watched pertinent game films. The night before the game, Bernie Parrish's mental preparation paid off. Parrish was staying with the rest of the team at Cleveland's Pick-Carter Hotel, thinking of what he'd have to do against the Baltimore receivers. Suddenly, his attention was drawn to something in his notes from the previous night's movies of the Baltimore games. He had noticed that Baltimore receivers were the least effective when played tightly by defenders. Apparently, Parrish thought, Baltimore's passing attack was based more on the timing with which the plays were executed than the individual patterns. He passed on this important information to his teammates in the defensive secondary.

Even on the day of the game the Browns were reminded that most people thought they had no chance against Baltimore. In the morning papers they read that the Colts were a heavy favorite to win. And later, as fullback Brown walked to his car in a parking lot near the hotel, a group of Baltimore fans recognized him and jeered. "Laugh champs," they taunted. "Marchetti will rub your face in the dirt." Gino Marchetti, of course, was the Colts' All-Pro defensive end.

As the Browns sat in the locker room, they were thinking about what had been said about them. There was, they knew, only one way to make people change their minds. Coach Collier realized that, too. He didn't need to give pep talks. "It's time to go out and loosen up," he said. "There's really nothing for me to say. You know what you have to do." And with that the Browns charged onto the field.

The first period was scoreless. The Cleveland linemen successfully harassed Unitas so that he did not have time to find his receivers. When he did have time, he discovered that Cleveland's secondary had his targets covered as if by a blanket. Six minutes after the opening kickoff, Unitas was trapped attempting to pass and had to run. He gained seven yards, but the Browns did not mind. They were discovering that, if they could prevent Unitas from passing, he would not hurt them by running.

In the second period, Baltimore started driving hard, and the 79,544 fans in Cleveland's Municipal Stadium waited for the inevitable—the Unitas touchdown pass. It never came because linebacker Costello intercepted at the Cleveland 30. At half

Protected from Colt defensemen by guard John Wooten, Ryan has enough time to find a receiver.

In midair, Collins snares a pass from Ryan.

time, the score was still 0-0, and in the press box a sportswriter quipped, "Never have so many people paid so much money to see so little."

After intermission, the Browns started to give the fans their money's worth. Early in the third quarter, Lou Groza—with a 17-mile-an-hour wind at his back—kicked a 43-yard field goal, and the Browns led, 3-0.

Shortly after, Kanicki broke through the Colts' pass defense to spill Unitas for a two-yard loss and stall any chance of a Baltimore drive. Then the Browns took the ball and began to move. Starting at the Cleveland 36, Brown ran 46 yards to the Colts' 18. Cleveland now had a chance to break open the game. Ryan called for Collins to head for the end zone.

Collins did, and the pass was perfect. Touchdown! Groza kicked the extra point to make the score, 10-0. It seemed that the laugh champs were having the last laugh.

The next time the Browns got the ball, Ryan took to the air again. Collins was his receiver, and Gary grabbed the pass on the 15 and dashed into the end zone for a 42-yard touchdown. Cleveland 17, Baltimore 0. Ryan and Collins were making people forget that Unitas and Berry were supposed to be the best passing combination in pro football.

The Browns went into the third quarter with a 17-point lead, but they weren't finished scoring yet. Groza added a 10-yard field goal to widen the gap to 20 points. Then Ryan hit Collins with another pass for a 51-yard touchdown, the third of the afternoon. The final score was 27-0.

It had been a superb exhibition of football. The defensive unit of the underdog Browns had shut out the third highest scoring team in NFL history. In the locker room afterwards, linebacker Fiss was saying, "When he [Unitas] started to run, I knew we would win. He can't beat you with his legs."

Parrish was satisfied, too. "Were we tall enough out there today?" he asked with a grin. "We won

The great Jim Brown attempts to make his way through a mass of Colt tacklers.

five in a row early in the season and no one thought we were short. Then we lost some games, and I began to feel like a midget because people started to write that the Brown secondary was too short. We grew a few inches this afternoon."

The secondary was not the only unit of the Cleveland team that grew with victory. The members of the defensive line gained stature around the league—especially Kanicki. "Our defensive line played as hard and as good as we've ever played," said Glass. "The big thing that helped us was that Jim Kanicki played better than he ever played in his life."

Hearing the praise, Kanicki smiled and made a mental note to see his supermarket manager on Monday. The other Browns were going to enjoy the satisfaction of proving people wrong, too, Collins especially. He had won a car given by *Sport* Magazine to the title game's most valuable player. When someone asked him if he would give Ryan a ride in it, the beaming Collins said, "Shoot, the whole team deserves a ride. Everybody did just a great job today. Nobody will be calling us the laugh champs any longer."

Index

Page numbers in italics refer to photographs

About the Author

Phil Berger, formerly an editor with *Sport* Magazine, is a freelance writer who contributes regularly to *Sport, Dare* and *The National Observer*. His home is in New York City.

THE PUNT PASS AND KICK

NFL

LIBRARY